CORNWALL'S OWN

JOHN VAN DER KISTE

The History Press

Also by John Van der Kiste

A Divided Kingdom
A Grim Almanac of Devon
Childhood at Court 1819–1914
Cornish Murders (with Nicola Sly)
Crowns in a Changing World
Dearest Affie (with Bee Jordaan)
Dearest Vicky, Darling Fritz
Devon Murders
Devonshire's Own
Edward VII's Children
Emperor Francis Joseph
Frederick III
George V's Children
George III's Children
Gilbert & Sullivan's Christmas
Kaiser Wilhelm II
King George II and Queen Caroline
Kings of the Hellenes
Northern Crowns
Once a Grand Duchess (with Coryne Hall)
Princess Victoria Melita
Queen Victoria's Children
Somerset Murders (with Nicola Sly)
Sons, Servants and Statesmen
The Georgian Princesses
The Romanovs 1818–1959
William and Mary
Windsor and Habsburg

First published 2008

The History Press
The Mill, Brimscombe Port
Stroud, Gloucestershire, GL5 2QG
www.thehistorypress.co.uk

British Library Cataloguing in Publication Data.
A catalogue record for this book is available from the British Library.

ISBN 978 0 7509 5088 6
Typesetting and origination by The History Press
Printed in Great Britain

Contents

Preface & Acknowledgements

This book aims to draw together brief lives of over 100 of the great, the good and the legendary from all walks of Cornish life, past and present. All were either born in Cornwall or have spent much of their lives in the county and made a name for themselves there.

Reasons of space preclude adding a full bibliography of works consulted. The *Daily Telegraph*, the *Guardian*, *The Times*, the *Western Morning News*, and the *Oxford Dictionary of National Biography* have proved invaluable, and other online sources have been supplemented by a wealth of printed works where available.

Particular thanks are due to Sheila Tracy and Miles Tredinnick, for supplementing the information on themselves I already had. Special thanks must go to my wife Kim, for suggesting many names for inclusion, for reading the manuscript in draft form and assisting with illustrations; to my mother Kate, who took a keen interest in the work in progress but sadly died before it was complete; to Beth Hall at The History Press; and to my editor, Matilda Richards, for commissioning the work and helping me to see it through the press.

Picture Credits

Thanks to Catherine McCarthy for the photograph of Miles Tredinnick; Sheila Tracy for that of herself; Phil Wright for that of Charles Causley's grave; Tony Atkin and www.geograph.org.uk for that of Goonamarris Down; and Roland Godfrey for that of Brenda Wootton.

All other pictures are either from the author's collection or else in the public domain.

John Couch Adams

Mathematician and Astronomer

John Couch Adams was born at Lidcot, Laneast, on 5 June 1819, son of Thomas Adams, a tenant farmer. From an early age he demonstrated a remarkable aptitude for performing mathematical calculations in his head without the use of pen and paper. In October 1839 he entered St John's College, Cambridge, graduating with a BA in 1843.

While he was an undergraduate, his interest in astronomy led him to look more fully into certain unexplained irregularities in the motion of the planet Uranus, which he considered might be due to the action of a remote undiscovered planet twice as far from the Sun as Uranus. He worked out the calculations in his head before writing them down, and once he had committed them to paper, he submitted them to Professor James Challis, Director of the Cambridge Observatory, and George Biddell Airy, Astronomer Royal, at the Greenwich Observatory. Neither acknowledged his work at first, and some months later a French astronomer, Urbain Le Verrier, submitted similar work to the Director of the Berlin Observatory. He initially tried to claim the credit, but after Challis and Airy somewhat belatedly studied Adams's calculations it

was apparent that both astronomers had independently reached the same conclusion. The newly discovered planet was at first named Leverrier, then changed by general consent to Neptune.

A self-effacing man, Adams was offered a knighthood in 1847 but declined it, partly out of modesty and partly as he felt he did not have the means to maintain the lifestyle which would be expected of a man with such a title. The Royal Society awarded him its Copley Medal in 1848, and to mark his achievements the members of St John's College founded an Adams Prize to be awarded biennially for the best treatise on a mathematical subject. In 1851 he became President of the Royal Astronomical Society, and Pembroke College elected him to a lay fellowship which he held for the rest of his life. In 1858 he became Professor of Mathematics at St Andrews, but lectured only for a session, and vacated the chair for the Lowndean Professorship of Astronomy and Geometry at Cambridge. Two years later he succeeded Challis as Director of the Observatory, a post he retained for life.

The post of Astronomer Royal was offered him in 1881, but he preferred to continue teaching and research in Cambridge. He was British delegate to the International Prime Meridian Conference at Washington in 1884, when he also attended the meetings of the British Association at Montreal and the American Association at Philadelphia. When a private collection of Newton's unpublished mathematical writings was donated to Cambridge University, Adams and a colleague undertook to arrange the material, publishing a catalogue in 1888. Although best remembered for the discovery of Neptune, he also accomplished much important work on gravitational astronomy and terrestrial magnetism, including the publication of new tables of the moon's parallax.

In 1863 he married Eliza Bruce. He died at the Cambridge Observatory on 21 January 1892. John Passmore Edwards (q.v.) erected a public institute in his honour at Launceston, and he is also commemorated with a memorial tablet in Westminster Abbey.

An Gof (Michael Joseph) and Thomas Flamank

Rebel Leaders

Michael Joseph (better known as Michael An Gof, *An Gof* being Cornish for 'blacksmith') was born in St Keverne, where he became the village blacksmith. Thomas Flamank's father, Richard, was an important tin producer and property owner in Bodmin, and in 1492 Thomas was MP for Bodmin. Otherwise, prior to the 1497 rebellion, little is known about their lives.

The Cornish were angry when King Henry VII levied new taxes to finance an invasion of Scotland, intended to force King James IV to surrender or expel the pretender Perkin Warbeck from his country. Flamank argued that such a measure was illegal as it was the business of the north, and the north alone, to defend the Scottish border. Additional levies at this time were seen as particularly unjust as the bedrock of the Cornish economy, tin production, was in decline. Moreover the Council of Prince

Arthur, Duke of Cornwall, was trying to impose new regulations on local industry, thus incurring the wrath of Cornishmen who resented interference in the workings of their regulatory body, the Stannaries. The regulations were ignored, and King Henry VII suspended the Stannary government, thus inflaming Cornish sensibilities even further.

In the early summer of 1497 Joseph led a march beginning at St Keverne, joining with Flamank and his supporters at Bodmin. Their adherents were an enthusiastic band of men, women and children, with no military training or arms, only bows, arrows and agricultural implements with no proper staff to organise accommodation and supplies on the march. They fended for themselves, living off the land and finding any available shelter at night. At Wells, Somerset, they were joined by Lord Audley, a disaffected nobleman who now became their titular leader, and marched on across England towards London without meeting resistance. In Kent they hoped to gain support from the area of the focus of Jack Cade's rebellion of 1450, but they knew the King had been recruiting, training and equipping his army which was by then about 25,000-strong against perhaps no more than 15,000 Cornishmen. This, and the lack of supplies and arms demoralised the army, and desertion began in earnest. Those who were left reached Blackheath on 16 June, where they were confronted by King Henry's army and the ill-equipped and untrained Cornish forces shrank to about 8,000. It was deployed to dominate the River Thames at Deptford Strand, thus attempting to threaten communication and trade with London.

On 17 June they were surrounded by the King's army and fought bravely in a pitched battle at Deptford Bridge, but had no chance against such a large well-equipped enemy. They were defeated and least 200 were killed. Flamank and Audley were captured while An Gof fled to Greenwich, but he was captured as he fled into the Friar's Church and sent to the Tower of London. A week later in the White Hall at Westminster he and Flamank were condemned to death. On 27 June 1497 they

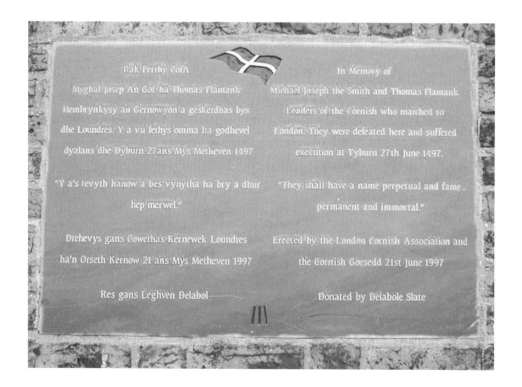

were hanged, drawn and quartered at Tyburn and their heads displayed on pikestaffs on London Bridge. Just before his execution, An Gof said he would have 'a name perpetual and a fame permanent and immortal', while Thomas Flamank remarked, 'Speak the truth and only then can you be free of your chains'. The twenty-seventh June is still celebrated as An Gof Day, with annual events in Bodmin, St Keverne, and London dedicated to the memory of both men.

John Arnold

Watchmaker

John Arnold was born in Bodmin in 1736, the son of a watchmaker, also called John. Intent on following the same profession, he was apprenticed to his father and became a partner at their premises just off Fore Street, a place since renamed Arnold's Passage, with a commemorative plaque marking the spot. He also worked briefly for his uncle William Arnold, a gunsmith. Around 1755 he went to the Netherlands where he improved his knowledge of clockmaking and learned German.

Returning to England about two years later, he earned his living as an itinerant mechanic for a while until he repaired a repeating watch for William McGuire of St Albans, who lent Arnold the money to set up his own business in the City of London. He opened his first shop at Devereux Court, The Strand, in May 1762, specialising in small timepieces, and his reputation as a skilled watchmaker grew quickly. In 1764 he was introduced at court and presented King George III with a miniature watch set in a ring, at the time the smallest repeating and striking watch ever made. The King bought it from him for £500, the first of several payments he was to receive for royal services.

In 1767 he began to manufacture marine timepieces. One was much admired by Captain James Cook, who used it on his second voyage to the southern Pacific Ocean in 1772–1775. Arnold now had a rival, Thomas Earnshaw, who was also producing similar artefacts in significant quantities. Partly to meet such competition, he devised a way of simplifying the design which enabled him to keep his prices down. Among his innovative design features were the temperature compensation using a bimetallic strip, and his solution to the problem of friction in the balance spring, for which he obtained a patent in 1776. He also made several fine regulator clocks for observatory use, as well as general domestic clocks and watches which he sold to private customers, as well as to the British Admiralty and the East India Co. From 1779 he ran his workshops and resided at Well Hall, Eltham. In 1783 he became a member of the Clockmakers' Co.

His son John Roger Arnold was born in 1769, and from about 1783 he was apprenticed to both his father and the French watchmaker Abraham Louis Breguet. Father and son went into partnership in 1787, trading as John Arnold & Son. In 1788 they produced a new pocket timepiece. The Astronomer Royal tested it at Greenwich, and was so impressed that he decided to give it a new name, the chronometer, thus becoming the first person to use that term in its modern sense.

In 1792 John the younger went to Paris to work with the clockmaker Abraham Louis Breguet, but the state of revolutionary France soon made it advisable for him to return to London. After his father retired in 1796 his son continued to run the business at the Cornhill shop. The elder John died at his home, Well Hall, Eltham, on 25 August 1799 and was buried at Chislehurst beside his wife, who had predeceased him. Their son John Roger continued the business after his death with John Dent, and became Master of the Worshipful Company of Clockmakers in London in 1817.

Henry Bastian

Biologist, Physician and Neurologist

Henry Charlton Bastian was born in Truro on 26 April 1837, the third of five children of merchant James Bastian. As a child he was fascinated by natural history, and among his early publications were papers on the flora of Falmouth and surrounding parishes and a collection of the ferns of Great Britain. He was an authority on free nematode worms and named 100 new species in *A Monograph on the Anguillulidae or Free Namatodes* (1864). For this he was elected Fellow of the Royal Society in 1868, but he had to give up this interest after developing an allergy to the worms. He then devoted his career to clinical neurology.

After attending University College, London, he worked at St Mary's Hospital, Paddington, received his MD in 1866, and returned to the college the following year as Professor of Pathological Anatomy. In 1868 he was elected a fellow of the Royal Society of London, and was a physician in nervous diseases at the National Hospital, Queen Square, from 1868 to 1902. In 1878 he was promoted to physician at University College Hospital, where he later held the chair of medicine, served as a censor of the Royal College of Physicians of London from 1897 to 1898, received an honorary fellowship of the Royal College of Physicians of Ireland and an honorary MD degree from the Royal University of Ireland. From 1884 to 1898 he was Crown referee in cases of supposed insanity.

The publication of several papers and treatises on speech disorders and associated conditions from the earliest days of his career added to his medical reputation. In 1869 he published a seminal paper on various forms of speech loss and their relation to cerebral disease, his approach to the understanding of aphasia being based on a theory that independent centres in the brain controlled speech and vision. It was followed by other studies including *The Brain as an Organ of Mind* (1880), *On Paralyses: Cerebral, Bulbar and Spinal* (1886), *On Various Forms of Hysterical or Functional Paralysis* (1893), and *Treatise on Aphasia and other Speech Disorders* (1898).

His other great interest was that of the origins of life. He had been intrigued by the problem of abiogenesis, or spontaneous generation, since around 1865 when he defended the doctrine by both logic and experiment. Mainstream biological opinion assumed that life always came from life and that the actual origins if not the creation of life occurred at some distant time. During debates in the 1870s on the experimental demonstrations of the phenomenon and standing of the germ theory of disease, he maintained that certain bacteria could survive boiling, and this led to improved sterilisation procedures in bacteriological research. Contrary to accepted scientific opinion, he believed there was no strict boundary between organic and inorganic life. He argued that since living matter must have arisen from non-living matter at an early stage in evolution, such a process could still be taking place. His theories and biological studies were expounded in several works including *The Modes of Origin of Lowest Organisms* (1871), *The Beginnings of Life* (1872), *Evolution and the Origin of Life* (1874), *Studies in Heterogenesis* (1901–4), and *The Nature and Origin of Living Matter* (1905).

In 1866 he married Julia Augusta Orme, and they had four children. Late in life he was awarded a Civil List pension of £150 a year in recognition of his services to science. He died at his home at Chesham Bois, Buckinghamshire, on 17 November 1915.

Sir John Betjeman

Poet, Journalist and Historian

John Betjeman was born on 28 August 1906 in Highgate, London, the son of a cabinet maker. The family name of Betjemann was altered during the First World War to sound less Germanic. He was educated at the Dragon School, Oxford, Marlborough College, and Magdalen College, Oxford, where he failed his divinity exams and left without a degree. For a while he worked as a private secretary and then as a schoolmaster at a preparatory school. His verse autobiography, *Summoned by Bells* (1960), told the story of his boyhood and early adult life up to this time.

In 1930 he became assistant editor of *The Architectural Review*, and from then on was a tireless champion of Victorian and Edwardian art and architecture. The following year he published *Mount Zion,* his first book of poems. Throughout his career he produced several volumes of verse, as well as books on architectural and art history, and guide books, including the *Shell Guides* to Cornwall and Devon.

In 1941 he and his wife went to Dublin where he worked as press officer to the British Embassy, and it was later revealed that the IRA considered assassinating him because they were convinced he must be a spy – until they read his poetry and decided he could not possibly be one. Two years later he returned to England to work in the Ministry of Information. After the war he resumed his writing, and also established a reputation as a regular commentator on radio and television, for which he made documentaries such as *Metroland* and *A Passion for Churches.*

His father had owned several properties at Trebetherick, near Polzeath, and childhood holidays with his parents marked the start of what would be a lifelong attachment to north Cornwall. He would regularly visit the area throughout his adult life, and he and his wife Penelope often took the children there on short breaks as well. Having always hankered after owning his own house at Trebetherick, the success of *Collected Poems* (1958) and *Summoned by Bells* enabled him to fulfil this dream, and in 1960 he purchased Treen for £8,000 as a holiday home. He contributed a short essay to *Both Sides of the Tamar: a West Country Alphabet* (1975), in which he called Trebetherick 'the happiest place for childhood that anyone could have ... it may have been a suburb by the sea and for all our crabbing, fishing and bathing, nothing to do with the real Cornish who regarded us as the foreigners we still are.'

He was awarded a CBE in 1960, knighted in 1969, and appointed Poet Laureate in 1972. By the time of the publication of *A Nip in The Air* (1974), another volume of poetry, his health was beginning to fail, with Parkinson's Disease, strokes and heart trouble leaving him increasingly enfeebled. In May 1984 he made his final journey to Trebetherick, where he died on 19 May. It had previously been arranged that an ambulance would take him back to London the previous day, but his daughter Candida was convinced that he was not keen on the idea: 'I know that at that point he decided he wanted to die at Treen.' He was buried on 22 May at St Enodoc's Church, where a slate headstone marks his grave.

Frederick Betts

Army Officer and Ornithologist

Frederick Nicholson Betts was born in Launceston in 1906 and educated at Winchester College between 1920 and 1924. After leaving school he went to work in the tea plantations of Ceylon and later in the coffee plantations of Coorg, southern India. Joining the army in India, he rose to become a Captain in the Punjab Regiment, and in 1940 he was posted to Eritrea. On promotion to Lt-Col (Intelligence), he served in the V Force in Burma, a guerrilla and intelligence unit in north-eastern India which worked with the Assam Hill tribesmen. Here he met Ursula Graham Bower, an anthropologist studying the Nagas, and they were married in 1945.

In 1946 the Indian government appointed him political officer of the Subansiri region between the Assam plains and the McMahon Line, which marked the boundary between India and Tibet. Among his first duties was to establish a supply drop zone and set up a supply deposit for government offices in the region. In 1948, after India's declaration of independence, he and his wife moved to Kenya where he served in the veterinary service in the Western Masai Reserve and she became a coffee farmer.

Throughout his life he had been fascinated by ornithology. While working in India before the Second World War he devoted much of his free time to the study of bird life, and he was one of the first Europeans to do so at close range, reporting on species from the remote Khru Valley and parts of north-east India and Africa. In India he was an active member of the Bombay Natural History Society. The pioneering studies he made of the birds of Coorg, around this time led to a major work on the subject which he published in the society's journal.

His efforts were regarded as ahead of his time in that the entire study was based purely on his own observations of birds in the wild, and not merely on collected skins, which had often been the practice with earlier ornithologists. The extensive notes he made documented the differences in the avifauna of the dry and wet zones of Coorg, and also arrival dates for local and long-distance migrants. While he was living in Kenya he produced a widely acclaimed paper on the birds of Masai. Later he also took a keen interest in orchid cultivation.

In 1952 he, his wife and their two daughters returned to Britain, where they decided to make their home on the Isle of Mull in Scotland. Here he continued to spend his time studying birds and animals. In 1967 the family moved to Ringwood, where he became a member of the Hampshire Field Club's ornithological section and the Hampshire Naturalists' Trust. He was secretary of the New Forest Beagles, served on the New Forest Consultative Panel, and was a treasurer of the Burley Branch of the British Legion.

He died after a stroke while riding in the New Forest on 22 August 1973. His widow, who published several works on anthropology under her own name and a novel as Hugh Paterson, died in 1988.

William Bickford

Inventor

William Bickford was born in Ashburton, Devon in January 1774. Moving to Cornwall as a young man, he worked as a leather merchant at Truro, and then as a currier at Tuckingmill. The latter town was then in the heart of the Cornish mining industry, and though he had had no previous connection with the trade, he was concerned by the prevalence of miners' injuries, often fatal, which were caused by existing methods of setting off explosives to break up large amounts of rock. Many of these, he was convinced, were accidents that were occurring because of faulty or unreliable fuses, and though Cornish mines did not suffer from explosive gases, large numbers of men were killed by misuse of gunpowder. Early fuses were generally tubes of reeds filled with powder and extremely unreliable, either exploding too early and not giving miners time to get away, or taking too long to ignite and killing men who assumed the fuse must have gone out. He decided to put the explosive into a parchment cartridge to which he attached a small parchment tube containing powder as a safety fuse, though this proved unreliable and no safer than methods already in use.

One day in 1831 he visited his friend James Bray who owned a rope factory in Tolgarrick Road. He watched the rope makers twisting the separate strands together and realised that he might be able to adapt this process to make a fuse; a strand of yarn, impregnated with gunpowder could be included in the rope to make a reliable, predictable fuse. That same year he designed and took out a patent on the machine, which wound strands of rope around a central core of gunpowder, then wound another layer in the opposite direction in order to prevent the rope from untwisting. Finally the rope was varnished to make it waterproof. When one end was lit, the rope safety fuse burnt along its length at a steady rate, and it never went out. The shot-firer could cut off the right length of fuse to give himself time to escape from the resulting explosion.

Having perfected his methods, Bickford opened a factory at Tuckingmill where the devices could be made. The invention encountered initial resistance as the older, unpredictable fuses were cheaper, but at length the mining industry saw the advantage of adopting the safety fuses. In its first year, the Bickford factory in Tuckingmill made 45 miles of fuse, a huge amount as only a few feet were used for each blast. A hundred years later the same factory, which had been enlarged, made 104,545 miles of fuse.

Bickford became paralysed the year after his great invention and died in 1834. The remains of his factory are now occupied by a number of small businesses grouped around a courtyard beside the main crossroads in Tuckingmill. Over the years the basic process of making the fuse has remained virtually unchanged. Bickford-Smith & Co. left Cornwall and took their operation to America in 1836, and the safety-fuse manufacturing facility in Simsbury, Connecticut later became The Ensign-Bickford Co.

Samuel John 'Lamorna' Birch

Painter

Samuel John Birch was born in Egremont, Cheshire, on 7 June 1869, son of John Birch, a house painter and decorator. During childhood he moved to Manchester, and left school to work for an oilcloth manufacturer. Encouraged by his mother, he began to paint in his spare time, and exhibited his first picture at the Manchester Art Gallery when he was only fifteen. Four years later he moved to Halton, near Lancaster, where he worked in a mill, while continuing to paint during his spare time before and after working hours.

From 1889 onwards he had regularly visited Cornwall, where he became friends with, and was greatly influenced by, Stanhope Forbes (q.v.), who had settled at Newlyn in 1884 and who, with his wife Elizabeth, would found the Newlyn School of Art in 1899. Several other *plein air* artists had recently been attracted to the area because of the bright light and the relaxed atmosphere of the fishing village. On Forbes's recommendation, Birch went to study at the Académie Colarossi, Paris, for several months in 1896. In 1897 he settled at St Buryan, and five years later moved to Lamorna, near Penzance. As there was already an artist named Lionel Birch living in Newlyn, Birch acted on a suggestion made by Forbes and took the additional name of Lamorna in order to avoid any possible confusion between both men. In 1902 he married Emily Vivian, one of his pupils, and they had two daughters.

Lamorna provided him with endless inspiration for his landscapes, especially because of his passionate interest in rivers. He set up a studio near the river at Lamorna, half a mile from Lamorna Cove, later moving to Flagstaff Cottage at the head of the bay. He painted in the open air, often beginning soon after daybreak, working in both oils and watercolours. His river pictures testified to his fascination with the portrayal of flowing water, while his landscapes, with deep, dramatic skies and gilded clouds were especially popular. Several series of greetings cards and fine-art prints were made from his work.

The majority of his painting was done in Cornwall, but he was also a keen fisherman and made frequent visits to Scotland, Wales, the north-west of England as well as the West Country to paint and fish. Because of the latter activity he was sometimes known as the 'The Fisherman Artist', and according to fellow artist Sir Alfred Munnings, 'When he was not painting he was fishing; when he was not fishing he was painting'. Each summer he and his wife went on a river-based holiday, usually in Scotland but sometimes in Austria. He exhibited over 200 pictures at the Royal Academy from 1905 onwards, held his first one-man exhibition at the Fine Art Society in 1906, and also showed his work with the Royal Society of Painters in Watercolours, at Glasgow Institute of Fine Arts and at the Walker Art Gallery, Liverpool.

Throughout his seventy-year career he produced more than 20,000 pictures. He died at Lamorna after a stroke on 7 January 1955.

Henry Bone

Painter

Henry Bone was born at Truro on 6 February 1755, son of Henry Bone, a cabinet maker and carver. The family moved to Plymouth, where he learned to paint on hard-paste china for the Cookworthy factory. He continued his apprenticeship with Richard Champion in Bristol until the firm went bankrupt in 1779, and then moved to London with one guinea in his pocket and £5 borrowed from a friend, working on jewellery design and enamelling watches and fans.

After beginning to paint miniatures he began to exhibit them at the Royal Academy in 1781. One of his first portraits was a miniature on ivory which he had painted two years earlier of Elizabeth Van der Meulen, a descendant of Philip Van der Meulen, battle painter to William III, whom he married in January 1780. They had several children; the eldest, Henry Pierce Bone, became almost as famous as his father, and two grandchildren, all of whom went on to enjoy successful careers as miniaturists.

Bone tended to work by visiting private collections where he would carefully draw the chosen picture in pencil on to squared paper, or borrow pictures from the artist or owner and take them back to copy in his studio at 15 Berners Street. He used these drawings for several enamels of various sizes, notching the paper to allow accurate alignment, laying it over another paper coated with red chalk, and tracing through to the prepared enamel plaque, usually copper or brass, which he then fired to fix the chalk outline. Sometimes he traced the outline in ink on to transparent paper. The number of firings varied from six or seven to twelve or occasionally more, and the whole process sometimes took up to three years to complete. Most of the pictures he chose for enamel copies were religious and mythological subjects. He was also employed by Philip Rashleigh (q.v.) to produce paintings of some of his minerals for use in his published works. He was appointed enamel painter to the Prince of Wales in 1800, and later successively to George III, George IV, and William IV, elected an associate of the Royal Academy in 1801, and Royal Academician in 1811.

Towards the end of his career he undertook two major projects. The first was a series of portraits of the Russell family, commissioned by the Duke of Bedford and copied from portraits at Woburn Abbey, mostly in 1823 and 1824. The second was a set of eighty-five 'portraits of illustrious characters in the reign of Queen Elizabeth'. The latter were valued at £10,000 and he offered them to the nation for £4,000, but it was declined. They were exhibited at his Berners Street studio after his death, and again at the British Institution, where they were sold by Christies in 1836. A group of forty kings and queens from Edward III to Charles II, by Henry Bone and his son Henry Pierce Bone, was acquired for the Royal Collection.

He died in Clarendon Square, Somerstown, London, on 17 December 1834. His son became enamel painter to Queen Adelaide, widow of William IV, and Queen Victoria.

William Borlase

Antiquary and Naturalist

William Borlase was born on 2 February 1696, son of John Borlase, MP for St Ives, and his wife, Lydia, at their home, Pendeen House, St Just. He was educated in Penzance and Plymouth and in 1713 he entered Exeter College, Oxford, where he graduated BA in 1716 and proceeded MA in 1719. He was admitted into deacon's orders by the Bishop of Exeter in 1719, ordained the following year, became rector of Ludgvan from 1722, and also held the living of St Just from 1732. He married Anne, daughter of the Revd W. M. Smith, rector of Camborne and Illogan, in 1724 and they had six sons, two of whom died in infancy.

Throughout his life he was a keen collector of minerals and fossils, and friends whom he sent various specimens encouraged him to make a study of Cornish natural history. This led to a particular interest in ancient Cornish monuments, and in the religion and customs of ancient Britons before their conversion to Christianity. In these projects he was helped by his friend the Revd Edward Collins, vicar of St Erth, and by his wife, who helped with collecting and recording samples. He sent samples of the minerals he found, including tin, copper, iron, and lead ores, to his friend John Andrew, an Oxford physician, who went to Leiden in 1735 to study under the Dutch naturalist Herman Boerhaave. Andrew passed samples to Boerhaave, Carl Linnaeus, and J.F. Gronovius, and Borlase had regular correspondence with the last.

Through an introduction by their mutual friend William Oliver (q.v.) of Bath, Borlase also supplied samples of Cornish minerals to the poet Alexander Pope, who decorated the grotto in his garden at Twickenham, where he erected an inscription to Borlase.

In 1748 he befriended the Revd Dr Charles Lyttelton and Jeremiah Milles, both influential members of the Society of Antiquaries of London, who assisted and encouraged him in his work on Cornish natural history and antiquities. That same year he began a correspondence with Emanuel Mendes da Costa, a London naturalist and mineralogist, who visited him in 1749 to study mines and geology. In 1750 da Costa successfully proposed him for fellowship of the Royal Society after his essay on 'Spar and Sparry Productions, called Cornish Diamonds', and also put him in touch with the antiquarian William Stukeley, who shared his fascination with ancient religion.

In 1753 he went to Oxford to supervise the printing and publication of his *Observations on the Antiquities Historical and Monumental, of the County of Cornwall*, the first chronological account of the antiquities of the county, and the first book to describe, illustrate, and classify a significant number of them. Around the same time he and his friend Henry Usticke went to the Isles of Scilly, where they studied stone circles and rock basins. His research was published in the *Philosophical Transactions*, and later in *Observations on the Ancient and Present State of the Islands of Scilly* (1756). Between 1752 and 1757 he travelled around Cornwall gathering material for a topographical survey of the county. His book *The Natural History of Cornwall* was published at Oxford in 1758, after which he donated his collection of fossils, minerals, and antiquities to the Ashmolean Museum, Oxford. He died at his home in Ludgvan on 31 August 1772.

Edward Boscawen

Naval Commander

Edward Boscawen was born at Tregothnan, near Falmouth, on 19 August 1711, the third son of Hugh, 1st Viscount Falmouth. He joined the Royal Navy at the age of twelve, and was appointed a midshipman in 1727 while serving in the West Indies. In 1730 he distinguished himself at the taking of Porto Bello. Throughout his career at sea, he became known to his men as Old Dreadnaught and Wry-necked Dick.

His reputation rests largely on the role he took in the War of the Austrian Succession, fought between 1740 and 1748. At the siege of Cartagena in March 1741 he led a party of seamen to take a battery of fifteen 24-pound cannon, while under fire from another fort. Soon after his return to England in the following year he became MP for Truro. In 1744 he captured the French frigate *Médée*, the first ship to be taken in the war. In May 1747 he distinguished himself in the first Battle of Finisterre, and was wounded in the shoulder with a musket ball, but all ten French ships were taken. In July he was made Rear-Admiral and Commander-in-Chief of the expedition to the East Indies. Later that month he arrived off Fort St David's, and soon after laid siege to Pondicherry, but the sickness of his men and the approach of the monsoons led to the raising of the siege.

Soon afterwards peace was declared and Madras was surrendered to him by the French. In April 1750 he returned to England; in the following year he was made one of the Lords of the Admiralty, and an Elder Brother of Trinity House. At around the same time he bought and rebuilt Hatchlands Park, Surrey.

In April 1755 he intercepted the French squadron bound to North America, and took the *Alcide* and *Lys* of sixty-four guns each, returning to Spithead with his prizes and 1,500 prisoners. In 1758 he was appointed Admiral of the Blue and Commander-in-Chief of the expedition to Cape Breton, when he and General Amherst took the fortress of Louisburg, and the island of Cape Bretons. His brother Col. George Boscawen commanded the 29th Regiment of Foot also at Fortress Louisburg. In Nova Scotia he was invited to attend the colonial council, and he may have been involved in a decision that led to the mass expulsion of 10,000 Acadians, or the deportation of the indigenous French-speaking population, in 1755.

His greatest victory came in 1759 as France was planning to send an invasion force from Brest, but needed to rendezvous its fleet to protect the force during the crossing. After he was appointed to the Mediterranean command he pursued the French fleet, and after a sharp engagement in the Battle of Lagos took three large ships and burnt two, returning to Spithead with his prizes and 2,000 prisoners. The victory prevented France from assembling a fleet to cover their planned invasion.

In December 1760 he was appointed general of the marines, with an annual salary of £3,000, and was also sworn a member of the Privy Council. He died of a fever on 10 January 1761 at Hatchlands Park, and is buried in a tomb in St Michael's churchyard, Penkivel. The town of Boscawen, New Hampshire is named after him.

Billy Bray

Preacher

William 'Billy' Trewartha Bray was born on 1 June 1794, in Twelveheads in the parish of Kea, halfway between Truro and Redruth. His father died when he was seven, and he went to live with his grandfather, who had helped to build the Methodist chapel at Twelveheads. After he left home for Devon in 1811 at the age of seventeen he went to work in the tin and copper mines, turned to drink and lived what he later called 'a bad life.' In his own words, he claimed, 'I became the companion of drunkards, and during that time I was very near hell'. When he returned to Cornwall in 1818 he was spending all the money he earned on ale. Twice he had a lucky escape from death. One was in an accident in the mines, and the other was when he and a drunken companion decided to ride a horse which they found in the road; it stumbled against a stone, fell and almost crushed them.

In 1821 he married a local girl, Joanna, a lapsed Christian. At first having a wife to support made little difference to his way of life, and for the next two years he continued to spend most of his wages on beer. Everything changed in November 1823 when he came across a copy of John Bunyan's *Visions of Heaven and Hell*. Waking early one morning he knelt by his bedside, asking God to save his soul. On the next pay day he returned from the mines sober, having vowed to give up alcohol and tobacco. Friends thought it would only be a matter of time before he went back to his old ways, but they were proved wrong. He became a devout Christian, started to live by his faith, became a man of prayer and worship, and regularly preached in the local Bible Christian chapels. He was a frequent speaker at meetings, urging his fellow miners and neighbours to follow him and come to Christ.

At first his clothes were of poor quality as he had spent so much on drink. The Quakers proved generous, and one of them gave him the coat off his back. It was said that he never met a person without inquiring as to the condition of his soul, and that he had a shouting religion. 'I lift up one foot and it says, "Glory!", he said, 'and I lift the other foot and it says, "Amen!" and so they keep on like that all the time I'm walking.'

In his *Journal*, written in 1864, he told the story of his conversion and the reaction of his workmates with whom he used to spend many a happy evening drinking and telling dirty jokes. He wrote about the three chapels, Bethel, Kerley Downs and Great Deliverance, which he built while still working up to twenty hours a day down the mines.

An enthusiastic and sometimes unconventional preacher, he was sometimes regarded as too fervent. When his wife died, he cried out, 'Bless the Lord! My dear Joey is gone up with the shining angels!' During his last illness the doctor who was attending him told him he would not recover. 'Glory, glory be to God!' he exclaimed. 'I shall soon be in heaven.' Next he then asked the doctor whether he should tell them that 'you will be coming too?' He died on 25 May 1868 and was buried at Baldhu Church, where a monument to him (pictured) was erected.

W.J. Burley

Author

William John Burley was born in Falmouth on 1 August 1914 and educated at Truro Technical School. He served a five-year apprenticeship at the Truro Gas Co., where he was promoted to become technical assistant in 1936 and assistant manager two years later. In 1940 he was appointed manager of the Okehampton Gas Co. Being in a 'reserved' occupation he was not called up to serve in the army, but served as a sergeant in the Home Guard.

Similar managerial appointments to gas companies at Crewkerne and Camborne followed, but soon after the war he was looking for a career change. He had become increasingly interested in entomology and zoology, and made a detailed study of insect life around the river at Reskadinnick. In 1950 he resigned his post with the gas company and obtained a scholarship at Balliol College, Oxford, to study zoology, obtaining a second class honours degree three years later. That same year, 1953, he worked briefly at Tiffins School, Kingston, and was then offered the post of head of biology at Richmond & East Sheen County Grammar School. In 1955 he obtained a similar position at Newquay Grammar School, where he remained until retiring in 1974. When the grammar schools were closed he moved with the staff and pupils to Treberras Comprehensive School, where his wife Muriel was the headmaster's secretary. For much of this time, he was also the careers master.

While teaching, he realised he 'was not going to have a very handsome pension', and decided to try his hand at authorship. Detective fiction was a very popular genre in the 1960s and he started writing in his early fifties. His first book, *A Taste of Power,* featuring amateur detective Dr Henry Pym, was published in 1966. Two years later Superintendent Charles Wycliffe made his first appearance in *Three Toed Pussy.* A second Henry Pym title, *Death in Willow Pattern*, followed in 1969. He also wrote a science-fiction novel, *The Sixth Day* (1978), as well as a Gothic romance, *Charles and Elizabeth* (1979), and two other murder stories, *The Schoolmaster* (1977), and *The House of Care* (1981). Altogether he published twenty-eight titles.

Nevertheless the Wycliffe books, of which there would be twenty-two in all, proved the most popular. In 1993 Wycliffe became a household name when one of the stories was dramatised for television in a pilot episode starring Jack Shepherd in the title role. It was an instant success and five series, comprising thirty-five episodes all shot on location in Cornwall, were shown over the next five years. By the end *Wycliffe* was attracting a regular weekly audience of 10 million viewers.

Burley was a member of the Crime Writers' Association, but according to fellow crime writer Martin Edwards, he apparently took little if any part in its activities. He was essentially a private man, happiest in the company of family and close friends; the impression he gave was that of 'a self-contained man who scorned fashion and PR, and [who] preferred to let his fiction speak for itself'.

In 1956 he and his wife bought a home at Holywell, near Newquay. Here he was working on what would have been the twenty-third book in the series, *Wycliffe's Last Lap*, when he died on 15 November 2002.

Rowena Cade

Founder of the Minack Theatre

Rowena Cade was born on 2 August 1893 in Spondon, Derbyshire, great-great-granddaughter of the painter Joseph Wright ('Wright of Derby'). The second of four children, at the age of eight she took the title role in her mother's production of *Alice Through the Looking Glass* with a cast of eleven local children, and two performances with audiences of twenty-seven and forty-three respectively. This love of the theatre never left her, and she put it to good use when she moved to Cornwall.

In 1929 and 1930 a local village group of players had staged Shakespeare's *A Midsummer Night's Dream* in a nearby meadow. They decided their next production would be *The Tempest* for which she offered them her garden at Minack House, near Porthcurno. There was nowhere to seat an audience, but they were able to use an area on the opposite side of the bay. Within about six months Rowena and two assistants, her gardener Billy Rawlings and his mate Charles Thomas Angove, built a simple stage and some rough seating, hauling materials down from the house or up via the winding path from the beach. Such granite as was available was cut by hand from a pile of tumbled boulders, and stones were inched into place. However granite was too expensive to purchase in quantity, so she developed a technique for working with cement, decorating surfaces with lettering and intricate Celtic designs with the tip of an old screwdriver before they hardened. The terraces were in-filled with earth, small stones and pebbles shovelled down from the higher ledges, above a gully with a rocky granite outcrop jutting into the sea (*minack* in Cornish means stony or rocky place), on the slope above a sheer drop into the Atlantic.

The first performance of *The Tempest* in summer 1932 at the new theatre, staged with the sea as a backdrop, was lit by batteries, car headlights and power from Minack House, with the audience collecting tickets at a table in the garden before clambering down the gorse-lined path. Its reputation was made and it flourished each summer until closed in 1939 for the duration of the war. When evacuee children came from London, she became the local billeting officer. In 1944, the theatre was reopened briefly for use as a location for the Gainsborough Studios film *Love Story*, starring Stewart Granger and Margaret Lockwood, but bad weather forced them to retreat to a studio mock-up.

After the war she decided to separate the theatre from her garden by building walls, an access road, a car park and a flight of ninety steps up from the beach. Once she single-handedly carried twelve 15ft beams from the shoreline up to the theatre. Customs men looking for material from a recently wrecked Spanish freighter met her on the beach and asked if she had seen any missing timber. She admitted she had taken some wood that morning and invited them to come and see it. As they thought such a frail-looking woman could not possibly have removed what they were searching for, they declined and went on their way. 'I didn't tell them a lie now, did I?' she remarked to one of her assistants as they were putting the beams into position afterwards.

As takings from each short season did not cover her running costs, she had to cover all financial losses herself. In 1976 the theatre was registered as a charitable trust and was later run by a local management team. The trustees extended the season of plays, built a visitor centre open all year round and enlarged the retailing operation. With larger audiences, at last the theatre could pay its way. She died on 26 March 1983.

Reginald Pole Carew

Member of Parliament

Reginald Pole Carew was born on 28 July 1753, eldest son of Reginald Carew of Stoke Damerel, Plymouth. He succeeded to the Antony estate at Torpoint in 1772, and over the years enlarged it greatly with the purchase of additional properties. From his early adult life he was a regular traveller abroad, particularly throughout eastern Europe and Russia. Among those he met on his journeys was the philosopher and social reformer Jeremy Bentham, who praised him as 'a man certainly of great abilities, a vast stock of knowledge from all opportunities I have had of judging, of a most excellent heart'. In 1784 he married Jemima Yorke. The following year he bought a house in Berkeley Square, where he lived until moving to Cavendish Square in 1801.

Entering Parliament, he represented Penryn from 1782 to 1784, Reigate from 1787 to 1790, then Lostwithiel until 1796, and Fowey until 1799. In that year he resigned his seat to take office as Commissioner for Auditing Public Accounts, but resigned this appointment in 1802 when he became MP for Fowey a second time. In 1803 he briefly became Under Secretary of State for Home Affairs in the government under Viscount Addington.

In 1804 his wife and one of his sons died, leaving him with a small son and five daughters. In January 1805 he became a Privy Councillor. He was re-elected MP for Fowey in 1806 and Lostwithiel in 1812. In 1808 he married the Hon. Caroline Lyttleton.

In 1827 he published a pamphlet on the Corn Laws, and took an active part in debates on issues such as these, and the abolition of slavery, and parliamentary reform, culminating in the Reform Act of 1832.

Though such matters required his regular presence in London, he also spent much of his time when he could at Antony House with his wife and family, taking part in local

discussions and attending to business on the house, gardens and estate. Such an active life must have suited him very well, for in 1799 he had written to Addington, 'there is nothing of which I have a greater horror than that of being a partially idle man'. He became a Fellow of the Royal Society in 1788 and joined the Royal Institution in 1800. He had a passion for archaeology and scholarship, built a new library at Antony House, and became a Fellow of the Society of Antiquaries. In Cornwall he followed keenly the latest developments in agriculture, and was a subscriber to the Cornish Agricultural Society. Torpoint's position as a thriving business community owed much to his personal spirit of enterprise and devotion to the town's welfare. He died on 3 January 1835.

John Carter

Smuggler

John Carter was born in 1770 at Breage, near Helston. Known as the 'King of Prussia', he was the most successful and notorious smuggler of the Penzance district between 1777 and 1807, aided by his younger brothers, Harry and Charles. They ran an efficient and profitable smuggling operation for about thirty years.

The war against France had involved additional taxation, particularly on imported and luxury goods such as wine, spirits and tobacco, but owners of small fast boats could evade taxes if they could give customs officials the slip. Cornwall was a suitable smuggling base as it was so remote, and the area was a magnet for wreckers as well as smugglers. The Carters' home at Porthleah (originally called thus but renamed Prussia Cove (pictured) because of John's admiration for Frederick the Great, King of Prussia) was under a sheltered headland at the centre of Mount's Bay, with slipways for landing goods, as well as cellars and lofts where they could store their recently landed contraband. Some of the caves were said to be connected with the house above by secret passages.

Despite his flouting of the law, such as the time when customs officials were trying to follow one of the Carters' vessels into Prussia Cove, and John fired on a revenue cutter from a gun battery on top of the cliffs, he had a reputation for fairness and honesty. Once during his absence the excise officers removed a recently arrived cargo of tea to the Penzance custom house. On his return he and his men broke into the house at night and carried off all the goods which he regarded as his, leaving the rest alone. The authorities knew who had broken in 'because he has taken nothing away that was not his own'.

The Carter brothers were well known along the French coast, and once during the war with France they were arrested and imprisoned in St Malo for a year. They owned two large vessels, a 19-gun cutter of 160 tons, and a 20-gun lugger, each with a crew of around thirty men. Each vessel was equipped with at least one smaller boat for inshore work.

Most of the local Cornish community regarded smuggling as a perfectly legitimate activity, and there was a network of people to store, transport and sell goods in distant markets. There were inevitable skirmishes between rival gangs, and Harry Carter noted one such incident around 1788 in which the bone of his nose was cut in two 'and two very large cuts in my head that two or three pieces of my skull worked out afterwards'. He fled and remained in hiding for three months until his wounds had healed.

John Carter and Harry were confirmed Methodists. They forbade swearing on their vessels, and Harry was said to have held Sunday services on the quayside for smugglers when he was in Roscoff.

In 1803 the Carters' house was sold by auction. A copper mine had been opened on the cliffs overlooking the cove, coal was landed to drive the mine's steam engine, and the wealth from mining gradually became more lucrative, as well as more legal, than smuggling. Harry retired to a farm nearby, and became a full-time preacher, while John apparently disappeared into obscurity. Other members of the family were said to have continued smuggling into the 1820s, but the authorities were becoming more vigilant. In 1825 the building of a coastguard station at Prussia Cove dealt a death blow to smuggling in the area.

Charles Causley

Poet

Charles Stanley Causley was born on 24 August 1917 in Launceston, the only child of a groom and gardener who died from wounds sustained in the First World War when Charles was seven years old. He went to work as a clerk in a builder's office at sixteen, and then for a local electrical supply company. In the late 1930s he published three one-act plays. He joined the navy where he served during the Second World War as a coder, an episode he later wrote about in a book of short stories, *Hands to Dance*.

Nevertheless, his naval experiences were to make poetry his first love; 'I think I became a working poet the day I joined the destroyer Eclipse at Scapa Flow in August, 1940,' he later recorded. 'Though I wrote only fragmentary notes for the next three years, the wartime experience was a catalytic one. I knew that at last I had found my first subject, as well as a form.'

After returning home in 1946, he studied English and history at teacher training college at Peterborough, then went back to teach at the same grammar school in Launceston where he had studied as a boy, and spent the rest of his life in Cornwall. He published his first collection of poems, *Farewell, Aggie Weston*, in 1951, *Survivor's Leave* followed in 1953, and was followed by several more. Apart from two visits to Perth as a visiting fellow at the University of Western Australia, he rarely left his home town. He was much in demand at poetry readings throughout England, broadcast regularly for the BBC, served on the poetry panel of the Arts Council from 1962 to 1966, and was visiting fellow in poetry at Exeter for a year.

In addition to poetry he also wrote two verse plays, stories and books for children, and compiled various anthologies. An intensely private person, he was nevertheless always approachable, and became a close friend of other writers including Siegfried Sassoon, A.L. Rowse (q.v.), Jack Clemo (q.v.) and Ted Hughes.

In 1958 he was made a Fellow of the Royal Society of Literature and was awarded a CBE in 1986. Between 1962 and 1966 he was a member of the Poetry Panel of the Arts Council of Great Britain; in 1973-74 he was Visiting Fellow in Poetry at the University of Exeter, where he received an honorary doctorate. In 1990 he was made a Companion of Literature by the Royal Society of Literature. Other awards he received included the Queen's Gold Medal for Poetry in 1967, a Cholmondeley Award in 1971, and the Heywood Hill Literary Prize in 2000. In the latter year he was made a Companion of Literature by the Royal Society of Literature, an award he greeted with the words, 'My goodness, what an encouragement!' There was an unsuccessful campaign to have him appointed Poet Laureate after the death of John Betjeman (q.v.) in 1984.

'All poetry is magic,' he wrote in an introduction to *The Puffin Book of Magic Verse* in 1974. 'It is a spell against insensitivity, failure of imagination, ignorance and barbarism.'

He died on 4 November 2003, and was buried in St Thomas's churchyard, Launceston, only a few yards from the spot where he was born. He never married, and never wrote an autobiography, saying that the truth about his life was in his poems.

Jack Clemo

Poet

Reginald John ('Jack') Clemo was born near Goonamarris (pictured), St Stephen, St Austell on 11 March 1916. His father, a clay kiln-worker, who was said by some to be 'a dissolute character', was killed on active naval service in the First World War. His mother Eveline was a dogmatic Nonconformist of unswerving faith. At the age of five he suffered the first of several temporary attacks of blindness; on leaving school at the age of twelve, he became something of a rebel, driven by demons and the contrasts of his parents' personalities, abandoning himself to daydreams and fitful, black moods. At around the age of twenty he became deaf. He was strongly associated both with Cornwall and his Christian belief. His work was visionary and inspired by the Cornish landscape. He began to write at the end of his schooldays, but for many years his only vehicle for publishing his verse and stories was a local newspaper.

In 1948 he published his first novel, *Wilding Graft,* and in 1949 an autobiography, *Confession of a Rebel.* His first volume of poetry, *The Clay Verge* (1951), featured one of his best-remembered poems, 'Christ in the Clay-pit'. Another collection that year, *The Wintry Priesthood,* won a Festival of Britain prize.

In 1953 he had an attack of cerebral paralysis and a year later he became permanently blind. He continued to publish further volumes of poetry, including *The Map of Clay* (1961), *Cactus on Carmel* (1967), *The Echoing Tip* (1971) and *Broad Autumn* (1975), as well as a theological study, *The Invading Gospel* (1958). In October 1968 he married Ruth Grace Peaty. *The Marriage of a Rebel,* his second volume of autobiography, was published in 1980. That year his early life was the subject of a BBC TV drama documentary, *A Different Drummer.* He was awarded a civil-list pension for services to literature in 1961. In 1970 he was made Prydyth an Pry (Poet of the Clay) at the Cornish Gorsedd, and in 1981 received an honorary doctorate of literature from the University of Exeter.

In 1984 Jack and Ruth left Cornwall and moved to Weymouth where his health improved and his poetry took on a more measured, calmer tone, taking in the Dorset landscape and engaging with characters from his Braille readings. He and his wife worshipped regularly at Weymouth Baptist Church. His second novel, *The Shadowed Bed,* appeared in 1986. In 1987 he visited Venice and in 1993, Florence. These trips inspired further verse, combining landscape and love with his Christian faith, and weaving the personal into the history of European literature. *Selected Poems* was published in 1988, followed by *Approach to Murano* in 1993.

He died of cancer on 25 July 1994 at Weymouth, and was buried there a week later. Charles Causley (q.v.), who had been best man at his wedding, called him 'one of the best landscape poets of his generation'. A final collection of poems, *The Cured Arno,* was published in 1995 and a novel, *The Clay Kiln,* in 2000. Trethosa Methodist Chapel, where he was baptised, married, and where he and his wife worshipped together, opened a room to his memory in 2001. His literary papers, including manuscripts of prose and poetry works, were deposited with the University of Exeter. There was much local anger in 2005 when a china-clay company demolished his former home in order to build laboratories on the site.

John William Colenso

Mathematician and Theologian

John William Colenso was born at St Austell on 24 January 1814. He read mathematics at Cambridge, where he gained his BA. In 1839 he went to Harrow School as mathematical tutor, but had few pupils, and also lost most of his property in a fire. Heavily in debt, he returned to Cambridge and restored his fortunes by further tutoring and the sale to Longmans of textbooks he had written on algebra and arithmetic.

In 1846 he became rector of Forncett St Mary, Norfolk, and in 1853 he was appointed first Bishop of Natal. He taught himself the Zulu language, compiled a grammar and a dictionary, and translated the New Testament and other portions of scripture into the language, as well as acquiring a printing press which he had installed his missionary station at Ekukhanyeni in Natal.

Before beginning his missionary career, he had published a volume of sermons indicating that he did not fully accept traditional biblical interpretation. His work with the Zulus gave him further food for thought, and in 1861 he published a commentary, *Epistle to the Romans,* in which he challenged the doctrine of eternal punishment, the view that Holy Communion was a precondition to salvation, and the theory that the ancestors of newly Christianised Africans were condemned to eternal damnation. Questions put to him by students in Natal encouraged him to re-examine the contents of the *Pentateuch* and the Book of Joshua and question whether certain sections of these books should be understood as literally or historically accurate. His conclusions were published in a series of treatises on both books. The ensuing controversy in England provoked much dissent from clergy and laity alike who refused to accept the possibility of biblical fallibility, attracted the notice of continental religious academics and played an important contribution in the development of biblical scholarship.

His liberal views on the treatment of African natives angered the High Church Party in South Africa and in England, and the South African bishops headed by Bishop Gray, Metropolitan Bishop of Capetown, pronounced his deposition in December 1863. He refused to appear before this tribunal, sent a proxy protest, and appealed to the Judicial Committee of the Privy Council in London. The Privy Council ruled that the bishop of Cape Town had no authority to interfere with the Bishop of Natal.

His adversaries were unable to remove him from office, but succeeded in restricting his ability to preach both in Natal and in England. Bishop Gray excommunicated him and consecrated a rival bishop of Natal. The contributions of the missionary societies were withdrawn, but an attempt to deprive him of his episcopal income and the control of the cathedral was frustrated by another court ruling. Encouraged by a generous testimonial raised in England, to which many clergymen subscribed,

he returned to his diocese, and devoted the latter years of his life to further labours as a biblical commentator and translator. He also championed the cause of King Cetewayo and the rights of Zulus against Boer oppression and official encroachments during the Zulu War, thus making more enemies among the colonists than he had ever made among the clergy. He died at Durban on 20 June 1883.

Judith Cook

Journalist and Campaigner

Judith Anne Cushing was born in Manchester on 9 July 1933, the daughter of a mining engineer, and educated at Stretford Grammar School. She met her first husband Douglas Cook, then a music student, while she was working as secretary to Sir John Barbarolli, conductor of the Hallé Orchestra. They married in 1952 and moved from Essex to a cottage near Penzance.

After the Cuban Missile Crisis of 1962 and the threat of global nuclear war she wrote a letter to *The Guardian*, expressing her concern as a mother about bringing children into such a threatening world. The replies from over 2,000 other women sharing her concerns led to her founding the anti-nuclear protest body Voice of Women, through the columns of the *Guardian* women's page, and she visited Moscow and Washington with other campaigners to protest against nuclear weapons. She continued writing for the women's page throughout the decade, as well as for other national newspapers about environmental issues.

When her marriage broke up, she left Cornwall for the Midlands and full-time journalism. She became features editor of the *Birmingham Post*, and then worked for Anglia TV. Returning to Cornwall she settled in Newlyn with Martin Green, whom she had met in 1979. In 1981 she won the Margaret Rhondda Prize for services to the public through journalism after her work on the toxic herbicide 245T, and in the following year published *Portrait of a Poison: The 245T Story*. She was a member of the Crime Writers' Association, and the author of over thirty books, including thrillers and non-fiction. Her subjects included environmental and political issues, notably *Price Of Freedom* (1985), about access to information and medical records, *Red Alert* (1986), on the worldwide dangers of nuclear waste, and *The Year of the Pyres* (2001), on the disastrous effects of the foot and mouth disease outbreak on the farming community that year; biographies of people including the Elizabethan astrologer Simon Forman, J.B. Priestley, Daphne du Maurier (q.v.), and Mary Bryant, the Fowey highwaywoman; and theatre studies, including *Women in Shakespeare* (1980).

Her most famous book, *Who Killed Hilda Murrell?* (1985), examined the case of a well-known anti-nuclear campaigner, found murdered in a field near her ransacked Shrewsbury home in 1984, just before she was due to present a paper on the hazards of nuclear waste to the Sizewell-B nuclear power station inquiry. An article by Cook in the *New Statesman* suggested a political motive, citing various discrepancies in the police record of the crime-scene investigation.

Her second book about Murrell, *Unlawful Killing* (1994), linked her death to the Falklands War and controversy surrounding the sinking of the Argentinian cruiser, the *General Belgrano*, and a play about the affair which was presented at several small theatres.

She wrote for several amateur theatre productions, and her adaptation of *The Barchester Chronicles* was staged at the Chichester Festival Theatre. For a time she was Arts Council resident dramatist at the Theatre Royal, Plymouth, and part-time lecturer in Elizabethan and Jacobean theatre at Exeter University. She helped to found the amateur Rose Theatre Co., which staged productions in Penlee Park open-air theatre, Penzance.

Only four days after her wedding to Green, she died on 12 May 2004 after suffering a stroke. Her last book, the thriller *Keeper's Gold*, was published two months later.

Selina Cooper

Political Activist

Selina Jane Coombe, the sixth of seven surviving children of Charles Coombe, a construction worker, was born in Callington on 4 December 1864. After the death of her father from typhoid, the destitute family left Cornwall to seek work in the north-west and settled in Barnoldswick, Lancashire, in 1876. At first she divided her day between school and the factory as a 'creeler', responsible for maintaining a constant supply of fresh bobbins for the cotton emerging from the card frames. At thirteen she began to work full-time, though this was interrupted when she had to stay at home and look after her ailing mother. On the latter's death in 1889 she returned to work and joined the Nelson branch of the Cotton Worker's Union. In 1891 she was involved in a trade-union dispute involving attempts to force employers to provide proper toilet facilities for women.

She joined the Independent Labour Party, and attended education classes organised by the Nelson Women's Co-operative Guild, whose aims included encouraging women to discuss issues outside their home life. After reading history extensively in her spare time, she developed a knowledge of politics, and bought medical books so she could advise fellow workers who could not afford to visit a doctor. In 1896 she married Robert Cooper, a local weaver, committed socialist and advocate of women's suffrage.

In 1900 she joined the North of England Society for Women's Suffrage, and helped organise a petition in favour of votes for women signed by women working in the Lancashire cotton mills. It attracted about 30,000 signatories and she was chosen as one of the delegates to present the petition to the House of Commons. A year later the Independent Labour Party asked her to stand as a candidate for the Poor Law Guardian elections, and although the local press campaigned against her she was elected. In furtherance of her campaign for women's suffrage, she spoke at the Labour Party's 1905 conference urging the leadership to support the movement, became a full-time NUWSS (National Union of Women's Suffrage Societies) organiser, and in 1910 was chosen as one of the four women to present their case to the Prime Minister, Herbert Asquith.

During the First World War she worked on committees organising relief work in Nelson. A pacifist, she refused to take part in army recruiting campaigns. After military conscription was introduced in 1916 she became involved in helping those men sent to prison for refusing to fight. In 1917 she persuaded over 1,000 women in Nelson to take part in a Women's Peace Crusade procession, which ended in a riot with mounted police being called in to protect her and her fellow-speaker Margaret Bondfield. In 1918 the NUWSS tried unsuccessfully to persuade the Labour Party in Nelson to choose her as their candidate in the forthcoming general election. She was however elected to the town council and became a local magistrate. In 1934 she was invited by the pro-communist Women's World Committee Against War and Fascism to join a small delegation to Nazi Germany to visit women prisoners. A supporter of the Popular Front in the late 1930s, in 1940 she joined the more marginal People's Convention initiated by the Communist Party, and was expelled from the Labour Party.

She died at her home on 11 November 1946. A plaque was erected on the side of 59 St Mary's Street, Nelson, where she had moved with her husband and their daughter in 1901.

John Cornelius

Roman Catholic Priest and Martyr

John Cornelius, sometimes known as John Mohun, was born at Bodmin in 1557, possibly a son of Gervase Cornelius and Maud (or Mary) Buckingham. His parents were Irish and, though living in relative poverty, were thought to have been descended from the O'Mahon family. His patron, Sir John Arundell of Lanherne, sent him to Oxford and he was elected a fellow of Exeter College in June 1575, but as a staunch Roman Catholic he was expelled by royal commission in August 1578. A year later he went to the English College in Rheims and the English College in Rome in 1580.

After being ordained deacon in October 1581 he preached in the presence of Pope Gregory XIII on the feast of St Stephen, 26 December 1581. In 1583 he returned to England and was received by Sir John Arundell. Although there are few details of his life for the next few years, he was reported to be living with Arundell at his house in Muswell Hill in March 1588. After Arundell died in January 1591 Cornelius accompanied his widow, Anne, daughter of Edward, 3rd Earl of Derby, and formerly widow of Charles, 7th Lord Stourton, to Chideock Castle, Dorset. By this time Cornelius's reputation as a preacher and exorcist was well known. According to the Jesuit John Gerard, he was:

> ...so famous in preaching that all Catholics followed him as children do their nurse when they long for milk, and the man so full of the Apostle's charity, that with one fervent speech in imitation of the offer which St Paul made to be *'anathema pro fratribus'*, he expelled a devil out of a person whom he was exorcising. I know the time and place where it was performed; and where another wicked spirit confessed in a possessed person that his fellow was cast out by Cornelius his charity.

On 14 April 1594 Sir George Trenchard, one of the local Protestant sheriffs, raided Chideock Castle, and after searching for several hours they found Cornelius hiding in a priest hole. Thomas Bosgrave, a Cornish gentleman and kinsman of Arundell, and two servants of the Arundell family, were taken into custody at the same time, accused of aiding and abetting him.

While held in captivity by Trenchard at Wolfeton House, Dorset, Cornelius met several leading Protestants including William Charke, said to be 'easily their leader and principal in the whole of the county', and engaged them in debate. He also had a long discussion with Sir Walter Raleigh, who promised to intercede with Elizabeth I on his behalf. At the end of April Cornelius was sent to Marshalsea Prison, London, where he was tortured, but refused to betray his benefactors.

In June he was remanded to Dorchester for trial, where he was found guilty of high treason for being a priest, entering the kingdom and remaining there, and his companions convicted of having rendered assistance to one whom they knew to be a priest. They were assured of a pardon if they promised to embrace Protestantism but refused, and paid with their lives at Dorchester on 3 or 4 July 1594. As he walked to his death, he kissed the gallows with the words of St Andrew, "O Cross, long desired", etc. On the ladder he tried to speak to the multitude, but was prevented. After praying for his executioners and for the welfare of the Queen, he was executed. The bodies were given a dignified burial by the Catholics.

Jonathan Couch

Naturalist and Doctor

Jonathan Couch was born in the Warren, Polperro, on 15 March 1789, the only child of Richard Couch. He was educated at Lansallos and Bodmin Grammar School, and at the London medical schools of Guy's and St Thomas's. After completing his studies, he returned to Polperro in 1810 where he settled for the rest of his life, combining his skill and practice as a doctor with an abiding passion for natural history. His primary interest was ichthyology but his interests also included general zoology, botany, geology, archaeology, Cornish folklore and local history.

His reputation as a scholar and naturalist rests largely on the four-volume *Fishes of the British Islands*, published between 1862 and 1865. It was the first on its subject to be illustrated in colour, and remains one of the seminal works on British fish, containing over 250 plates from original drawings by the author. Many of the specimens illustrated were brought to Couch by the fishermen of Polperro, and he kept them immersed in water, or ran a jet of water over them, in order to preserve their full natural colours before they had a chance to fade. Copies of some of his original drawings are still on display at Polperro's Heritage Museum. They were so painstakingly accurate that in later years scholars from succeeding generations were able to correct some of his mistaken identifications.

Throughout his life he kept a series of notebooks in which he noted his observations, a *Journal of Natural History,* which formed an important record of social and economic matters from 1805 to 1870. It was acquired by the Royal Institution of Cornwall, Truro, in the late nineteenth century.

From his home he maintained a lively correspondence with many leading scientists of the day throughout Britain and Europe. Some were able to help him with information on the less familiar species, especially as his knowledge of the fishes of the northern fauna and particularly freshwaters was less certain. He inspired others with similar interests, and among his contacts was Thomas Bewick, who had himself planned but never published a book on British fishes.

He began a study of Cornish birds in or around 1829; it was never published during his lifetime, but saw the light of day over a century later. He also published work in several scientific and medical journals, and in other titles on subjects including religion and medicine. Other writings included his notes on Cornish beliefs, evolution, and a translation of Pliny's *Natural History*. A more personal account of his family and events in his life was published in the *Journal of the Royal Institution of Cornwall* in 1983.

He died at Polperro on 13 April 1870. His *History of Polperro* was published a year later, with an introduction by his son Thomas Quiller-Couch. Thrice married, one of his grandsons through his second marriage was the author Sir Arthur Quiller-Couch (q.v.).

Leonard Courtney

1st Baron Courtney of Penwith and Politician

Leonard Henry Courtney was born at Penzance on 6 July 1832, eldest son of John Sampson Courtney, a banker. After attending school locally he worked for six years in Bolitho's Bank at Penzance and then studied at Cambridge. In 1858 he was called to the bar at Lincoln's Inn, and spent six years as a barrister and freelance journalist. In 1865 he became a leader writer for *The Times*, writing over 3,000 articles for the paper during the next sixteen years, and a regular contributor to *Fortnightly Review*, mostly on political and economic topics. He was Professor of Political Economy at University College, London, from 1872 to 1875, was elected Liberal MP for Liskeard in 1876.

An anti-imperialist, he opposed British expansion in Africa, argued against government policy in Egypt, the Sudan, and South Africa, and opposed annexation of the Transvaal in 1877. In 1880 he was Under Secretary of State for the home department, in 1881 for the colonies, and in 1882 Secretary to the Treasury; but he was always a stubborn fighter for principle, and on finding that the government's Reform Bill in 1884 contained no mention of proportional representation, to which he was deeply committed, he resigned his office. He refused to support Gladstone's Home Rule Bill in 1885, helped to defeat it in Parliament, and joined the Liberal Unionists. After the electoral constituencies in Cornwall were redrawn, that same year he became MP for Bodmin. In 1883 he married Catherine Potter, an elder sister of Beatrice Webb, and prominent supporter of the women's movement.

In 1886 he was elected Chairman of Committees in the House of Commons, and became a Privy Councillor in 1889. Within a few years his increasingly radical views, especially on Irish politics and imperial issues, antagonised many of his fellow Liberal Unionists. After 1895 his divergences from the Unionist party on questions other than Irish politics became more marked. He denounced the Jameson raid of 1896, attacked the policies which led to the outbreak of the South African War in 1899, and sympathised with the Boers. During that conflict he was chairman of the South African Conciliation Committee, which opposed demands for annexation of the Boer states and unconditional surrender. He did not stand for re-election in 1900, and deteriorating eyesight made him consider withdrawing from public life altogether. Returning to authorship, in 1901 he published *The Working Constitution of the United Kingdom*, and three years later, anonymously, *The Diary of a Churchgoer*.

He rejoined the Liberal party, and unsuccessfully contested Edinburgh West at the 1906 general election. Later that year he was created Baron Courtney of Penwith. A regular speaker in the Lords, he disagreed with Sir Edward Grey's foreign policy, advocated armament reduction, attacked the Anglo-French entente and proposed a counter-balancing Anglo-German agreement. During the war he defended freedom of speech and conscience, and in November 1915 was the first Parliamentarian to call for peace negotiations as the only means of ending the war. He worked with the Union of Democratic Control to pursue justice for conscientious objectors. He died at his Chelsea home on 11 May 1918.

Nick Darke

Playwright

Nicholas Temperley Watson Darke was born on 29 August 1948 in St Eval, near Padstow, his father Bob a farmer, his mother Betty Cowan an actress. He was educated at Truro Cathedral School (until expelled for vandalising the cricket pitch) and Newquay, and trained as an actor at Rose Bruford College, Kent.

In April 1971 he joined the Victoria Theatre, Stoke, where he stayed seven years, acting in over eighty plays with parts ranging from classical drama to song and dance numbers. He also directed eight plays and wrote a pantomime script of *Mother Goose* and an adaptation of *The Scarlet Pimpernel*. The experience was invaluable, and he later said that 'the secret of how to write plays lies in performing, not writing them.'

Encouraged to concentrate on writing, he returned to Cornwall to pursue his vocation. His first original play, commissioned by the theatre's director Peter Cheeseman, was *Never Say Rabbit in a Boat* (1978). Several of his subsequent works were premiered by the Royal Shakespeare Co., the Royal Court Theatre, the National Theatre, and the local Kneehigh Theatre Co., founded in 1980 as a children's theatre group. They included more experimental, political plays, such as *Catch* (1981), based on the saga of two Cornish fishermen who, wrongfooted by European Community regulations, turn in desperation to smuggling cocaine. Its debut was followed two years later by its production as a radio play. *The Body* (1983) was a black comedy with an anti-nuclear message, and *Ting Tang Mine* (1987) a musical community play about rival Cornish mining villages in the depression after the Napoleonic Wars, a critical parable of capitalism. Among his most successful RSC productions were the comedy *The Dead Monkey* (1986), and *Kissing the Pope* (1989), based on guerrilla fighters in Nicaragua battling with the US-backed Contras. By the early 1990s he had found homes for his work at the National, the Bush and the Royal Court. Local issues featured in many of his plays, notably *The King Of Prussia* (1985), an eighteenth-century smuggling saga which reflected his views on second-home owners along the Cornish coastline, and *The Riot* (1999), inspired by the 1896 Sabbath riots when Newlyn fishermen demonstrated against Sunday fishing boats from Lowestoft.

Although business sometimes required his presence in London, he was always happiest back in his native county, preferably by the sea. Much of his life was spent in an old house made of Cornish stone on the beach at Porthcothan. An enthusiastic lobster fisherman and environmentalist, he would trawl the beach after heavy gales to collect wreckage, an interest which sparked a BBC TV film, *The Wrecking Season*, produced by his wife Jan, a film-maker and painter. They devoted much time together to coastal ecology and argued with the local council over attempts to tidy up the strand-line during the summer. Tourism, he wrote, was like tin mining, as it put Cornwall 'at the mercy of speculators and fortune hunters, and those who make the biggest buck are the landowners. Culture is debased and everything, including history, becomes a commodity.'

In 2001 a stroke left him unable to read, write or speak, yet he collaborated with Jane and producer Simon Elmes on *Dumbstruck*, a BBC Radio 4 documentary based on efforts to regain his voice literally and artistically. He died of cancer on 10 June 2005.

Mary Ann Davenport

Actress

Mary Ann Harvey was born at Launceston in 1759. She made her first professional appearance on the stage at Bath on 21 December 1784, as Lappet in Henry Fielding's *The Miser*. After two seasons in the theatre at Bath she played at Exeter and Bristol. At the latter she met George Gosling Davenport, a provincial actor, whom she married in 1786. They worked as itinerant strolling players prior to joining the Crow Street Theatre, Dublin, in 1792. One of her most acclaimed roles there was as Rosalind in Shakespeare's *As You Like It*. She also frequently played juvenile heroines in more contemporary drama, though she was accomplished enough to take the role of an old woman when required to do so.

The following year, husband and wife played together at the Covent Garden Theatre, where they had been engaged at the rate of £2 a week. In September 1794 she appeared as Mrs Hardcastle in Goldsmith's *She Stoops to Conquer*. The other roles she took during the season included those of Lady Wronghead in Vanbrugh's *The Provoked Husband*, the nurse in *Romeo and Juliet*, and the title role in Sheridan Knowles's *The Duenna*. Thereafter she divided the rest of her career between Covent Garden and the Haymarket Theatre, and generally spent some summer seasons at the latter. By 1825 she was earning around £12 per week. Her later roles included those of Dame Ashfield in Thomas Morton's *Speed the Plough*, Monica in William Dimond's *The Foundling of the Forest*, Deborah Dowlas in Colman's *The Heir-at-Law*, and Mrs Brulgruddery in Colman's *John Bull*.

Although her husband was also an actor by profession, he was generally considered to be the less talented of the couple. He was given lesser acting roles, and eventually his duties were confined largely to administration, in particular as secretary to the Covent Garden Theatrical Fund, until he retired in 1812. He died on 13 March 1814.

As a widow she continued to work on the stage for the next sixteen years, her last role being that of the nurse in *Romeo and Juliet*. She retired from acting in May 1830.

She died at her house in St Michael's Place, Brompton, London, on 8 May 1843, and was buried at St Paul's, Covent Garden. According to an obituary in the *Gentleman's Magazine*, July 1843, she had been living alone, and her children, a daughter, and a son with a post in India, had predeceased her.

Sir Humphry Davy

Physicist and Chemist

Humphry Davy was born in Penzance on 17 December 1778, son of a woodcarver, and educated in Truro. His brother John and cousin Edmund were also noted chemists. Their father died in 1794, and to help support the family Davy became an apprentice to a surgeon-apothecary in Penzance. In 1797 he took up chemistry and was taken on by Thomas Beddoes, as an assistant at his Medical Pneumatic Institution in Bristol, where he experimented with various new gases, discovered the anaesthetic effect of laughing gas (nitrous oxide), and published details of his research in *Researches, Chemical and Philosophical* in 1800. He was appointed as a lecturer at the Royal Institution and became a fellow of the Royal Society in 1803.

Through pioneering work done by other chemists, he understood that the production of electricity depended on a chemical reaction taking place, and his first researches on the subject were published in *On Some Chemical Agencies of Electricity* (1806). Through electrolysis he discovered new metals including potassium, sodium, barium, strontium, calcium and magnesium, and studied the forces involved in these separations, thus inventing the new field of electrochemistry.

He found that when he passed electrical current through some substances, these substances decomposed, a process later called electrolysis. His work led him to propose that the elements of a chemical compound are held together by electrical forces. At first, he tried to separate the metals by electrolysing aqueous solutions of the alkalis, but this yielded only hydrogen gas. He then tried passing current through molten compounds, and thus separated globules of pure metal.

In 1812 he was knighted, gave a farewell lecture to the Royal Institution, and married a widow, Jane Apreece. A year later he and his wife, accompanied by Michael Faraday as his scientific assistant and valet went to France to collect a medal awarded by Napoleon Bonaparte for his electro-chemical work. While in Paris Davy was asked to investigate a new substance which he found to be an element, now called iodine. After leaving Paris for Italy they went to Florence, where in a further series of experiments Davy and Faraday succeeded in using the sun's rays to ignite diamond, and proved that it was composed of pure carbon.

After their return to England in 1815, in response to requests from Newcastle miners telling of the danger they faced from methane gas which filled the mines, and which could be sparked off by the candles in their helmets to give them light in their work, he devised the 'Davy Lamp'. This used an iron gauze to enclose the flame, and thus prevent the methane from burning inside the lamp and passing out to the general atmosphere, thus allowing deep coal seams to be mined under safer conditions than previously. The principle of the safety lamp had already been demonstrated by William Reid Clanny and an engineer, George Stephenson, the latter claiming that he had come up first with the invention. Nevertheless Davy's use of gauze was soon copied by both inventors in their later designs.

In 1818 he was made a baronet, and two years later became President of the Royal Society. Six years later he had a stroke. In 1829 he made his home in Rome where he had a heart attack and died on 29 May in Geneva, Switzerland. He was buried in the Plain Palais cemetery in Geneva.

Gilbert Hunter Doble

Anglican Priest and Historian

Gilbert Hunter Doble was born at Penzance on 26 November 1880. His father, John Medley Doble, shared his enthusiasm for archaeology and local studies with his sons. A scholar of Exeter College, Oxford, he graduated in modern history in 1903 and then attended Ely Theological College. After his ordination in 1907 he served as assistant curate in various parts of England and Cornwall.

In 1919 he was appointed curate of the parish of Redruth, and from 1924 until his death he was vicar of St Wendrona Church, Wendron, near Helston. His Anglo-

Catholic leanings had been considered something of a bar to his preferment in the Church of England, and shortly before taking up his living at Wendron, a preferred appointment elsewhere had been suddenly withdrawn after he had given a public address on 're-catholicising Cornwall'. Nevertheless in 1935 he was appointed an honorary canon of Truro Cathedral.

During his ministry at Wendron he was devoted to children, especially those who had been deprived of proper care as a result of family poverty or through being placed in the workhouse. At the same time he pursued a lifelong study of sub-Roman Celtic Britain and Brittany, which had always been a major personal interest and on which he came to be regarded as one of the foremost experts. He was especially drawn to finding out more about the medieval *vitae* or 'lives' and legends, relating to the early Christian holy men and women (or 'saints') of Cornwall, Wales and of Brittany. His researches were published between 1923 and 1945 in a collection of forty-eight booklets, 'Cornish Saints Series', with the later issues from 1928 onwards including historical commentaries by Charles Henderson, a foremost county scholar of the age. They were later reissued in book form in one volume, minus the Henderson Commentaries. Until the publication of Orme's *Saints of Cornwall* in 2000, they were reckoned to be the most thorough and scholarly works on the subject, although with hindsight they have been regarded by some scholars as hagiography rather than objective assessments.

He also wrote and published a series of histories of Cornish parishes, and was an enthusiastic collector of Cornish folklore and folksong. In 1928 he was made a Bard of the Cornish Gorsedd, taking the Bardic name Gwas Gwendron (Servant of Gwendron) and was awarded the Jenner Medal of the Royal Institution of Cornwall. He was responsible for the first performance of the Cornish miracle play *Beunans Meriasek* since the Reformation in June 1924 (in English translation). It proved to be the first of many well-received productions of the drama, some of which were staged in the original Cornish language. His research also led to the revival of the Hal-an-Tow, an old Celtic traditional dance performed each May at the annual Helston Floral Day.

He died at Helston on 15 April 1945 and was buried in the churchyard at Wendron. His personal library and manuscript diaries were later deposited at the Courtney Library, Royal Cornwall Museum, Truro.

Daphne du Maurier

Author

Daphne du Maurier was born in London on 13 May 1907, daughter of the actor-manager and later writer Sir Gerald du Maurier and actress Muriel Beaumont, and granddaughter of caricaturist George du Maurier. Among her other ancestors was Mary Anne Clarke, mistress of the Duke of York, second son of King George III. In childhood she was a voracious reader. Her uncle, a magazine editor,

published one of her stories when she was in her teens and found her a literary agent. She was educated in London, Meudon, France, and Paris.

Her lifelong love affair with Cornwall began when she spent short family holidays there during childhood. In 1926 her parents bought a holiday home at Bodinnick, near Fowey, where she wrote her first book, *The Loving Spirit*, published in 1931. Major (later Lt-Col) Frederick Browning was so moved by reading the book that he sailed to Fowey to meet her – and in July 1932 they were married at Lanteglos Church.

Two further novels followed in quick succession, *I'll Never Be Young Again* (1932) and *The Progress of Julius* (1933), before she turned to writing about her father and her ancestors in *Gerald* (1934) and *The du Mauriers* (1937). Her reputation, however, rests primarily on her novels, most of which were set in Cornwall. *Jamaica Inn* (1936) and *Rebecca* (1938) were her most successful and have remained the most popular, partly through film and television adaptations. *Rebecca*, to some extent inspired by Charlotte Brontë's *Jane Eyre*, has itself inspired several sequels by other novelists in recent years.

During the first ten years of their marriage, Daphne and her family only spent holidays in Cornwall. In 1943 they moved there permanently in 1943, taking a twenty-five-year lease on Menabilly, a house overlooking the sea belonging to the Rashleigh family. Manderley, the setting for *Rebecca*, was in fact Menabilly.

Her subsequent novels included *Frenchman's Creek* (1941), *Hungry Hill* (1943), *My Cousin Rachel* (1951), *Castle Dor* (1961) with Sir Arthur Quiller-Couch (q.v.) who had left it unfinished at his death, *The House on the Strand* (1969), and her last, *Rule Britannia* (1972). Her short stories were published in several volumes including *Come Wind, Come Weather* (1940), *The Apple Tree* (1952), and *Not After Midnight* (1971). Two of these stories, *The Birds* and *Don't Look Now*, were filmed. In addition to adapting *Rebecca* for the stage, she enjoyed some success with the plays *The Years Between* (1945) and *September Tide* (1948). Some of her later books, notably *Mary Anne* (1954), about Mary Anne Clarke, and *The Glass-Blowers* (1963), blended fact with fiction, though they are considered as non-fiction. She returned to biography with *The Infernal World of Branwell Brontë* (1960), and *The Winding Stair* (1976), a life of Sir Francis Bacon, while *Growing Pains* (1977) was a memoir of her early days. Her passion for the county which she had made her home was reflected in *Vanishing Cornwall* (1967), in which she wrote of her 'Freedom to write, to walk, to wander, freedom to climb hills, to pull a boat, to be alone.' Altogether she wrote nearly forty books.

Her husband died in 1965. In 1969 she was awarded the DBE for services to literature. That same year, when the lease on Menabilly expired, she leased Kilmarin, another house from the Rashleigh family. She died on 19 April 1989. A pictorial memoir, *Enchanted Cornwall*, appeared posthumously in 1992.

Sir John Eliot

Member of Parliament

John Eliot was born at Cuddenbeak, Port Eliot, St Germans, on 11 April 1592, son of Richard Eliot and Bridget Carswell, and educated at Blundell's, and Exeter College, Oxford. He married Radigund Gedie in 1609, and they had five sons and four daughters. After studying law he entered Parliament as member for St Germans in 1614. In 1618 he was knighted, and in 1619 he was appointed Vice-Admiral of Devon, with responsibility for the defence and control of the county's commerce. Two years later he was appointed Justice of the Peace for Cornwall.

In 1624, entering Parliament as member for Newport, he demanded that Parliament's liberties and privileges, recently curtailed by King James I, should be restored, and in the first Parliament of King Charles I a year later he urged more rigorous enforcement of laws against Roman Catholics. At first he had been a supporter of the Duke of Buckingham, the Lord Admiral and a royal favourite, but the latter's incompetence and high-handed treatment of Parliament, which was considered a malign influence on the young inexperienced King, made a bitter enemy of Eliot. As Leader of the House, in 1626 he demanded an inquiry into the recent raid on Cádiz, a humiliating British failure. He openly attacked Buckingham and his administration, persuading the House to defer granting subsidies without question and to present a remonstrance to the King, declaring its right to examine the ministers' conduct.

In May he was among those who took Buckingham's impeachment to the Lords, and next day he was sent to the Tower. When the Commons refused to sit while Eliot and Sir Dudley Digges, a leading ally of his, were both in prison, they were released and Parliament was dissolved on 15 June. Eliot was dismissed from his office of Vice-Admiral of Devon, and in 1627 he was again imprisoned for refusing to pay a forced loan, but set free shortly before the Parliament of 1628. He spoke against arbitrary taxation, was foremost in the promotion of the Petition of Right, and continued his outspoken censure of Buckingham, who was assassinated shortly afterwards.

In February 1629 after a debate on the royal right to levy tonnage and poundage, the King ordered an adjournment of Parliament. The speaker, Sir John Finch, was held down in the chair by Denzil Holles and Benjamin Valentine while Eliot's resolutions against illegal taxation and innovations in religion were read to the House. Eliot and eight other members were sent to the Tower in March. He refused to answer in his examination, relying on his parliamentary privilege, and was imprisoned again. On 26 January 1630 he appeared at the bar of the King's Bench on a charge of conspiracy to resist the King's order, and refusing to acknowledge the jurisdiction of the court, was fined £2,000 and sent to the Tower until he agreed to submit, which he steadfastly refused. While in prison he wrote several works, including *Negotium posterorum*, an account of the 1625 Parliament, *The Monarchie of Man*, a political treatise, and *De jure majestatis, a Political Treatise of Government*.

In captivity he contracted consumption and died on 27 November 1632. When his son requested permission to move the body to St Germans the King refused, saying, 'Let Sir John Eliot be buried in the church of that parish where he died,' and he was interred at St Peter's Ad Vincula Church within the Tower.

Bob Fitzsimmons

Champion Boxer

Robert James ('Bob') Fitzsimmons was born in Helston on 4 June 1862 or 26 May 1863 (sources vary), youngest child of James Fitzsimmons, a constable in the local police. At the age of nine he and his family emigrated to New Zealand. On leaving school he went to work as a blacksmith at his brother Jarrett's forge, where he developed a powerful physique with a huge upper frame which proved invaluable in his sporting career. He was also known as 'Ruby Robert' because of his freckles, red hair and fair complexion. In 1880 he won an amateur boxing tournament run by British bare-knuckle fighter Jem Mace, who encouraged him to go professional. He moved to Australia three years later, settled in Sydney and continued to work as a blacksmith while continuing to box.

In 1890 he moved to the United States, becoming an American citizen in 1893. In January 1891 he won the world middleweight title by knocking out Jack Dempsey in thirteen rounds in New Orleans. After knocking Dempsey down at least a dozen times, the latter was in a bad way and Fitzsimmons begged him to quit. Dempsey refused, so Fitzsimmons completed the contest by knocking him out and carrying him to his corner.

Having defended his middleweight title against several other challengers, he became the world heavyweight champion at Carson City, Nevada in March 1897 when he knocked out the skilled and much heavier Jim Corbett in round fourteen. He lost the title in New York in 1899 when he was knocked out in the eleventh round by James Jefferies, thirteen years his junior. After briefly taking up wrestling with little success, he soon returned to boxing and a year later he challenged Jeffries in an effort to regain the heavyweight crown; Jeffries sustained fractures to his nose and cheekbones, but still knocked Fitzsimmons out in round eight.

He also starred in travelling variety shows, especially exhibition fights, and occasionally appeared on stage as an actor. In 1902 he published a book, *Physical Culture and Self-Defence*. According to film historians, his fight with Bob KO Sweeney was probably the first boxing fight ever filmed. In 1903 when the light heavyweight division was created, he was the first to win world titles at three different weights when he became the world light heavyweight champion. He held the title for two years, when he was defeated by Jack O'Brien, and conceded that 'his day had gone'. Though he still fought for the next nine years, age and failing physical powers counted against him and he retired for good in 1914. He was the first heavyweight champion boxer born in Britain, although he never fought there, and the only European born boxer ever to hold world titles at three different weights. In his later years he claimed that he had taken part in more than 350 fights during his career, though in the absence of full records this figure may be an exaggeration.

He was married four times, firstly in 1885 to Louisa Johns (whom he divorced in 1893), secondly in 1893 to Rose Julian (who died 1903), and thirdly in 1903 to Julia May Gifford. After divorcing her in 1915 he married Mrs Temo Slomonin, a Russian evangelist who persuaded him to join her as a travelling preacher. He died on 22 October 1917 of influenza in Chicago and was buried in Graceland Cemetery.

Mick Fleetwood

Drummer

Michael John Kells Fleetwood was born at Redruth on 24 June 1947. His father Mike was an RAF fighter pilot, and because of postings to Egypt and Norway the family spent much of his childhood in each country. After performing badly in exams, he left school at fifteen to move to London and live with his sister and her family while trying to pursue a career as a drummer. During the next five years he played in several bands, including The Cheynes, The Bo Street Runners, Shotgun Express (with Rod Stewart), and John Mayall's Bluesbreakers. While working with the latter, he met guitarist Peter Green and bassist John McVie, and after leaving Mayall, they formed Fleetwood Mac in 1967. Releasing their first album early the following year, they became the most commercially successful group of the late '60s British blues boom, with hit albums and singles including *Man Of The World*, *Oh Well* and the No.1 guitar instrumental *Albatross*. In 1969 they spent more weeks on the British singles chart than any other act.

The group then went through hard times on a personal and business level, with constant personnel changes which soon left Fleetwood and McVie as they only remaining original members; it was fortuitous that the group had taken its name from them. As Green and the other two original guitarists left at various times, new members joined and the style changed from blues to a more mainstream pop-rock style. Such was the scale of their problems at one stage that the group's manager

Clifford Davis formed another Fleetwood Mac, resulting in legal action (which Davis lost) and leading to Fleetwood taking over as manager of the genuine group for several years as well as continuing to play drums.

They left Britain and based themselves in the United States, and after a few poorly selling albums they were revitalised by the recruitment of duo Lindsey Buckingham and Stevie Nicks. Their most popular, *Rumours*, released early in 1977, became one of the best-selling albums of all time, with estimated worldwide sales to date of over 30 million copies. Despite problems with drink, drugs, affairs and acrimony between members of the group, plus their various solo projects, they continued to record and tour together, and it was largely his determination to continue which kept them from disbanding. In addition he had health problems; after suffering recurring bouts of hypoglycemia during concerts, in 1979 he was diagnosed with diabetes.

He recorded several 'solo' albums with personnel outside the group, including *The Visitor* (1981), *I'm Not Me* (1983), credited to Mick Fleetwood's *Zoo*, and *Something Big* (2004). As an actor he appeared in various films and television episodes with small roles in *The Running Man* (1987), *Star Trek: The Next Generation* (1989), and *Snide and Prejudice* (1997). He and singer Samantha Fox co-presented the 1989 BRIT Awards, transmitted live on television and remembered for several embarrassing gaffes which led to the ceremony being pre-recorded for the next few years. In 1990 he published an autobiography, *Fleetwood: My Life and Adventures with Fleetwood Mac*, in which he candidly discussed episodes of substance abuse and bankruptcy as well as his career and work with other musicians. He became an American citizen in 2006.

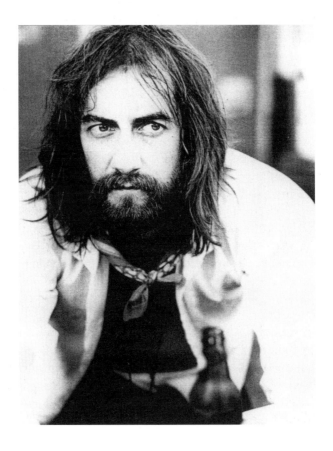

Samuel Foote

Dramatist, Actor and Theatre Manager

Samuel Foote was born into a wealthy Cornish family and baptised in Truro on 27 January 1721. His father John was Mayor of Truro and Member of Parliament for Tiverton. He was educated at Worcester and at Oxford, but expelled from the latter in February 1740 for insufficient attendance at classes. After studying law for a while, the lure of the good life tempted him away from serious work, and he was imprisoned for debt. On his release friends encouraged him to go onto the stage for a living, and he made his debut in *Othello* at the Haymarket Theatre in February 1744. He then played a summer season at the Theatre Royal, Dublin, and returned to London, taking comic roles in plays such as Farquhar's *The Constant Couple*, Vanbrugh's *The Relapse* and Villiers' *The Rehearsal*, all of which allowed him to display a gift of mimicry.

His extravagant lifestyle forced him to try and turn his fortunes around. He married Mary Hickes in January 1741, and soon squandered her generous dowry. Having decided to become a theatre manager, he took out a lease on the Haymarket Theatre in 1746, and assembled an acting company to write and stage *The Diversions of the Morning or, A Dish of Chocolate*, the first of several satirical revues based on mimicry of well-known personalities of the day. The 'dish' referred to the refreshments which he offered to accompany the entertainment onstage while the performance was given free of charge, a ruse designed to sidestep the restrictions of the Licensing Act. Similar productions followed, including *A Cup of Tea, The Auction of Pictures,* and *The Knights,* which made fun of Italian opera and the Cornish gentry, and earned him the title 'the English Aristophanes'.

At the close of the Haymarket season in 1749 he left London to visit Paris for three years. His next new comedy, *Taste,* produced at Drury Lane, mocked the art and antiquities market and aristocratic collectors, but only ran for five nights. He had greater success with *An Englishman in Paris,* in which he satirised the behaviour of English gentlemen abroad. Its success inspired fellow-playwright Arthur Murphy to write a sequel, *The Englishman returned from Paris.* Foote encouraged him, while secretly writing his own version which opened at Covent Garden in February 1756. Though he was accused of plagiarism, it ran regularly for several years. His next target was that of other writers and the condition of the 'starving writer' in *The Author* which premiered at Drury Lane in February 1757. During the next few years he worked at various times in Dublin and Edinburgh as well as London, his plays enjoying mixed success.

In 1766 he accepted a challenge to ride a particularly lively horse with the Duke of York. He was thrown, fractured a leg in two places and it was amputated, but he had two wooden legs made – one for everyday use and one for his appearances on stage. Next he was granted a patent for the Haymarket Theatre, Westminster, and in 1767 he built the new Haymarket Theatre, which he ran for ten years. In December 1776 he was charged in court with attempted homosexual assault, then a capital offence, but acquitted. Though he continued to appear onstage at the Haymarket, his health was failing. He was advised to spend the winter of 1777 in southern France; arriving at Dover on 20 October he caught a severe chill and died the next day. He was buried in Westminster Abbey.

Stanhope Forbes

Painter

Stanhope Alexander Forbes was born in Dublin on 18 November 1857, the son of William Forbes, a railway manager, and Juliette de Guise. William Forbes's brother, James Staats Forbes, was a keen art collector and friend of Josef Israels, a leading Hague School painter, and between them they probably inspired Stanhope to paint. He was educated at Alleyn's College, Dulwich, studied at the Lambeth School of Art and the Royal Academy Schools, then at a studio at Clichy, Paris in 1880, where he was encouraged by other painters to paint outside or *'en plein air'* in Brittany away from the scorching Paris summers. To him, the important thing was to obtain 'that quality of freshness, most difficult of attainment by any other means and which one is apt to lose when the work is brought into the studio for completion'.

For a while he considered a career as a portrait painter, but after he sold *A Street in Brittany* to the Walker Art Gallery, Liverpool, in 1881, he decided he would concentrate on: '*Plein Air* or nothing. It is the only way to achieve success. To stick at one branch of painting and make it your own'. In January 1884 he settled at Newlyn, which was about to become an unofficial centre for other artists of the *Plein Air* movement, notably Samuel John Lamorna Birch (q.v.). Newlyn's climate was mild enough for outdoor work most of the year, with unique light, endless new subjects of marine and village life. He was popular, sociable and good-natured, and soon became recognised as the informal president of artistic life in Newlyn.

He spent the first summer producing studies and smaller works, then painted his first large *Plein Air* work at Newlyn. *A Fish Sale on a Cornish Beach* was such a success at the 1885 Royal Academy exhibition that he followed it with similar canvases, including *The Slip* (1885), *Off to the Fishing Grounds* (1886), and *Their Ever Shifting Home* (1887), all typical of his pre-impressionistic qualities, though less well received by the public and the Academy. Ill-health forced him to turn to interior subjects, among them *The Village Philharmonic* (1888) which won a gold medal in Paris, *By order of the Court* (1890) and *The Health of the Bride* (1889).

In 1889 he married artist Elizabeth Armstrong, and they opened a school of painting in Newlyn a decade later which attracted several excellent students. He continued to paint, with works such as *Goodbye! Off to Skibereen* (1901), *Chadding in Mounts Bay* (1902) and *The Seine Boat* (1904) receiving great acclaim. From 1905 he painted less harbour and fishing scenes, turning more to farming, trade life and bucolic scenes, mostly still of a figurative nature. Between the wars he produced a series of Cornish townscapes.

Elizabeth died in 1912, and after her death he destroyed many of her letters, sketches and pastels. In 1915 he married Maudie Palmer, a former pupil of the school. That same year his son Alec joined the Duke of Cornwall's Light Infantry, was sent to the front line in August 1916, and died in the line of duty three weeks later. The quality of his work began to change; some later works lack the depth and dynamism he had achieved earlier and the *Plein Air* movement gradually became unfashionable as the remaining Newlyn painters embraced modernism and the St Ives school gained prominence. He died at Newlyn on 2 March 1947.

James Henry Fynn

Soldier and Victoria Cross Holder

James Henry Fynn was born on 24 November 1893 at St Clements in Truro, son of Frederick and Mary Baxter Fynn of Camborne. A few years later the family moved to Bodmin. After leaving school he went to South Wales seeking employment and worked as a coalminer at Cwmtillery.

On the outbreak of the First World War he enlisted with the 4th Battalion of the South Wales Borderers. He was one of 627 soldiers during the First World War who were awarded the Victoria Cross, for 'most conspicuous bravery, or some daring or pre-eminent act of valour or self-sacrifice, or extreme devotion to duty in the presence of the enemy', as the result of his action in Mesopotamia (now Iraq).

On 9 April 1916 at Sanna-i-Yat, Mesopotamia, he was awarded the Victoria Cross 'for conspicuous bravery' during the offensive in the Middle East. The *London Gazette* of 26 September 1916 recorded that after an attack during the night he was one of a small party of British soldiers which dug-in just in front of the advanced line and about 300yds from the enemy's trenches:

> Seeing several wounded men lying out in front he went out and bandaged them all under heavy fire, making several journeys in order to do so. He then went back to our advanced trench for a stretcher and, being unable to get one, he himself carried on his back a badly wounded man into safety. He then returned and, aided by another man who was wounded during the act, carried in another badly wounded man. He was under continuous fire while performing this gallant work.

Less than a year later, on 31 March 1917, he was one of several British soldiers killed in battle against the Turkish troops in Mesopotamia. His body was never returned to Cornwall, though he was remembered in an inscription carved on the headstone of his father, who died in 1942, in Bodmin Cemetery. A memorial, a roofed colonnade of white Indian stone, 80m long, with an obelisk 16m high as the central feature was erected at Basra, Iraq, to commemorate him and over 40,000 other British, Indian and West African soldiers who also perished in the operations in Mesopotamia between 1914 and 1921.

In 1966 a new housing estate in Bodmin was named Finn VC Estate in his honour, and the ceremony was attended by many members of his family and members of his Regiment. At the same time a commemorative plaque was unveiled opposite the library in Bodmin.

Guy Gibson

RAF Pilot and Victoria Cross Holder

Guy Penrose Gibson was born on 12 August 1918 in Simla, India, and his parents moved to Porthleven when he was three. Educated at Oxford, he joined the RAF in 1936. By the outbreak of the Second World War he was a bomber pilot with 83 Squadron. In July 1940 he was awarded the Distinguished Flying Cross on Bomber Command's first raid of the war. He then obtained a transfer to Fighter Command, thus avoiding the normal six-month rest from operations at a flying training establishment. As a night fighter pilot with 29 Squadron he claimed four kills in ninety-nine sorties and won a bar to his DFC.

He was promoted to Wing Commander and posted back to Bomber Command in 1942. During the next eleven months he led 106 Squadron, before taking over 617 Squadron. In February 1943 he was selected to command the new 617 Squadron and attack five hydroelectric dams in the Ruhr industrial area of Germany, with the bouncing bomb designed and developed by Barnes Wallis. It involved precision bombing and flying at night, something considered hazardous by even the most experienced pilots.

On the night of 16 May 1943 Bomber Command and Fighter Command both made several separate sorties over Germany and the Low Countries. Gibson led nineteen Avro Lancasters, each carrying one bomb. As 617 Squadron needed a full moon to carry out their mission, it was thought that the only way they could penetrate German anti-aircraft defences was to fly the whole mission as close to the ground as possible. They breached the Moehne Dam after five attempts, then Gibson led the three remaining Lancasters to attack the Eder Dam. Two other dams were attacked but not breached. Only eleven of the nineteen bombers survived the mission; fifty-three crew members died in the raid. Despite the resulting devastation the Germans managed to rebuild and recover more quickly than expected, but they were forced to use assets to protect key installations such as dams more than ever before.

He was awarded the Victoria Cross for his role in the Dambusters mission in recognition not just of the raid, but his leadership and valour demonstrated as master bomber on many previous sorties. His citation remarked that under his leadership, the squadron had 'executed one of the most devastating attacks of the war', and that 'throughout his operational career, prolonged exceptionally at his own request, he has shown leadership, determination and valour of the highest order'.

Soon afterwards he was sent on a lecture tour of the United States, mainly as the government wanted him kept out of the line of fire. He wrote *Enemy Coast Ahead*, a memoir of his wartime experiences, published two years after his death, and was chosen as prospective Conservative candidate for Macclesfield at the subsequent general election.

He returned to duty in June 1944. On 19 September he flew his De Havilland Mosquito as master bomber in a raid on Rheydt, but never arrived home. Later it was discovered that he and his navigator, James Warwick, had been killed when the plane crashed near Steenbergen, in the Netherlands. It was thought that he had been shot down, until investigators examined the wreckage, and found that because of a fault with the fuel tank selector, the aircraft had run out of fuel.

Davies Gilbert

Engineer, Author and Politician

Davies Giddy was born at St Erth on 6 March 1767, only child of Edward Giddy, curate of St Erth Church, and his wife Catherine. He was educated at Penzance Grammar School and by his father, and at Pembroke College, Oxford, studying mathematics, astronomy, and other sciences, and graduating with a MA in 1789. At Oxford he had become friends with Thomas Beddoes, reader in chemistry. Giddy advised Beddoes on the latter's Pneumatic Medical Institution in Bristol in which Humphry Davy (q.v.), whom Giddy had encouraged, was briefly employed.

Elected to the Royal Society in 1791, he served as its president from 1827 to 1830. He began a decade of county service in maintenance of public order, preparations to repel invasion, and control of food supplies, was High Sheriff of Cornwall from 1792 to 1793 and Deputy Lieutenant in 1795; he was president of the Penzance Agricultural Society. In 1814 he was a founder and first president of the Geological Society of Cornwall. He contributed a paper on the use of sea salt as manure to *Arthur Young's Annals of Agriculture*, and contributed to various journals including *Quarterly Journal of Science and Philosophical Transactions*.

He was MP for Helston in Cornwall from 1804 to 1806 and for Bodmin from 1806 to 1832. Though he refused office he chaired several parliamentary committees, drafting and shepherding many items of legislation on subjects such as finance, commodity prices, public works, weights and measures, the *Nautical Almanac*, the board of longitude, and the establishment of an astronomical observatory at the Cape of Good Hope. While he was most interested in Cornish concerns and scientific matters, he also took part in debates on major political questions, including agricultural protection and currency reform. During the Corn Bill riots of March 1815 his London house at

Holles Street was attacked by the mob. He voted consistently against any extension of the franchise, though in debates on the 1832 Reform Bill he supported its passage while still voting against the bill as a final gesture of support for a long held political principle. In 1832 he was awarded the honorary degree of DCL from Oxford.

In April 1808 he married Mary Ann Gilbert, and in December 1817 he took his wife's surname. Perpetuating it in this way enabled them to inherit a large estate at Eastbourne, Sussex, from her uncle who had no male heir. These estates passed to Giddy on the death of his wife's uncle in 1814 on the condition that the name of Gilbert be perpetuated; Davies Giddy became Davies Gilbert on 10 December 1817. He also inherited property in Cornwall on the death of his father.

He published a four-volume *A Parochial History of Cornwall* (1838), collected and published an edition of *Some Ancient Christmas Carols* in 1822, with a second edition in 1823, and two Cornish plays, *Pascon Agan Arluth* and *Gwreans an Bys*, which he called respectively *Mount Calvary* and *The Creation of the World*. In 1820 he was elected to the Society of Antiquaries. He died at Eastbourne on 24 December 1839 and was buried five days later in Eastbourne Church.

General Sir Walter Gilbert

Army Officer

Walter Raleigh Gilbert was born on 18 March 1785 at Bodmin, third son of the Revd Edmund Gilbert, vicar of Constantine and rector of Helland, Cornwall, and his wife, the daughter of Henry Garnett of Bristol. Through his father he was descended from Sir Humphrey Gilbert and the Devon family of Gilbert of Compton, and (as his forenames suggested) could claim another Elizabethan seafaring hero as an ancestor, as Sir Humphrey's mother was mother of Sir Walter Raleigh by a second marriage.

Most of his career was spent in India. In 1800 he became a cadet in the Bengal infantry, and was posted as ensign to the 15th Bengal Native Infantry in 1801. He was promoted to lieutenant in September 1803 during the Second Anglo-Maratha War, a conflict between the British East India Co. and the Maratha Empire in India. Under the leadership of Col. John Macdonald, he fought at the battles at Koil, Aligarh, Delhi, Laswari, the storming of Agra, and four unsuccessful attacks on the city and fort of Bharatpur, where he came to the favourable notice of General Lord Gerard Lake.

After the campaign he held other appointments including those of barrack-master and magistrate at Cawnpore, commandant of the Calcutta native militia, and commandant of the Ramgarh local battalion. He was promoted to captain in April 1810, major in 1820, lieutenant-colonel of the newly-formed 39th Bengal native infantry in 1824, colonel of the 35th native infantry in 1832, and major-general in June 1838. In June 1814 he married Isabella Rose, daughter of Major Thomas Ross, Royal Artillery, in Calcutta, and their son Francis was born two years later.

During the first Anglo-Sikh War of 1845-6 he commanded a division of the army under Sir Hugh Gough at the battles of Mudki and Ferozeshahr in December 1845, and at Sobraon two months later. In his dispatch Field-Marshal Hugh Gough, Cmmdr-in-Chief of India, praised Gilbert for his dedication, and he was awarded the KCB in April 1846. He also fought in the second Anglo-Sikh War, at the battles of Chilianwala in January 1849 and Gujrat the following month. The latter proved a conclusive British victory, as after the fighting he and his division pursued the remains of the Sikh army over the river Jhelum, and the defeated troops surrendered to him early in March. He pursued their Afghan allies to the entrance of the Khyber Pass. While in India he spent his leisure hours hunting and as a supporter of the turf. One day while out riding he dismounted when he found that his horse would not approach a large wild boar which was threatening the life of his friend, and charged the animal on foot with his spear.

He was appointed GCB in June 1849, a baronet in December 1850, lieutenant-general in November 1851, and was military member of the supreme council from December 1852 to February 1853. By this time years of overwork and the Indian climate had gradually taken their toll on his health. After a short spell in Egypt on medical advice he returned home in April 1853, and died at Stevens' Hotel, Bond Street, London, on 12 May. A memorial obelisk of granite 144ft high was erected at Bodmin, with details of his Sikh and Afghan campaigns inscribed on the four sides of the base.

John Glynn

Lawyer and Politician

John Glynn was baptized at Cardinham on 3 August 1722, second son of William and Rose Glynn. He entered Exeter College, Oxford, in 1738, but did not graduate, and was called to the bar at the Middle Temple in 1748. Within a few years he had established himself as one of the foremost barristers in London. In January 1763 he was created a Serjeant-at-Law, and undertook the role of counsel to the noted political maverick John Wilkes, of whom he became a prominent ally and defender. He also often acted on behalf of Wilkes, the radical publisher John Almon, and other government critics.

When Wilkes was elected MP for Middlesex in 1768 and promptly imprisoned on a charge of seditious libel, Glynn was chosen to stand in the subsequent by-election and won the seat in December after supporters of a pro-government candidate had violently interrupted the poll. This victory, achieved at a cost of £12,000, demonstrated the hold of Wilkes and his supporters on the county better than the success of the popular hero, as Glynn was merely his lawyer.

In the House of Commons he challenged an order by the government to deprive Wilkes of his Middlesex seat. During a debate in February 1769 on the matter, Horace Walpole observed that, 'Glynn gained great fame by the candour of his conduct on the whole proceeding; owning that, as counsel for Wilkes, he had maintained points which he would not assert in the House'. Outside Parliament he presided over a public meeting in 1769 that decided to establish a Society of Gentleman Supporters of the Bill of Rights in support of Wilkes, and he chaired a committee established to raise finance for the course. In the City of London the common council transferred the City's legal business from the official recorder to Glynn in 1770, and in November 1772 he was himself elected recorder by the court of aldermen, when the salary was raised from £600 to £1,000.

During the Falkland Islands crisis of 1770 the obstruction of naval press warrants by London radicals was criticised by Lord Chatham. Glynn went to consult him in person and devised a compromise solution of offering bounties for volunteers. He spoke regularly in Parliament between 1768 and 1774, usually on legal matters and the Middlesex election. His main interest was the rights of juries, especially in libel cases, and his most distinguished performance was a long speech in December 1770 in which he called unsuccessfully for an inquiry into the administration of justice, especially where the liberty of the press and the role of juries where concerned. In 1771 he spoke in favour of the freedom of the press to report on the regular Parliament. He spoke only once on America in 1774, but he voiced all the prejudices of London radicals against the Quebec Bill. He rose three times on the second reading in May 1774, speaking out against a measure for putting English subjects under French law, for not giving the colony a representative assembly, and for not safeguarding the Protestant religion. During the following month he spoke again, arguing in favour of jury trials.

At the 1774 general election Wilkes and Glynn were elected unopposed for Middlesex, and, from 1775 Glynn seconded Wilkes's annual motion to reverse the 1769 resolution declaring him ineligible to sit in the previous Parliament.

In 1763 he married Susanna Margaret Oglander, and they had four children. Suffering increasingly from gout in his later years, he died on 16 September 1779, and was buried at Cardinham a week later.

Sidney Godolphin

Poet and Courtier

Sidney Godolphin was baptised on 15 January 1610 at Breage, second of four children of Sir William Godolphin of Godolphin, an owner of mines at Godolphin and well-known for his mining expertise, and his wife Thomasine. As well as providing for the maintenance and education of his children, he left Sidney a large estate in Norfolk which would pass to him when he came of age.

In 1624 he was admitted as a commoner to Exeter College, Oxford., and in 1628 he was returned as MP for Helston. After travelling in France, the Low Countries and Denmark, he was invited to the royal court, where his friends included Edward Hyde, later Earl of Clarendon. He was also much admired as a poet, being a writer of songs and epitaphs, sonnets and epistles, a meditative chorus, a hymn, several short poems and a partial translation of Virgil's *Aeneid*. His hymn 'Meditation on the Nativity' has remained popular in anthologies over the years. His translation of Virgil's 'The Passion of Dido', which he undertook in conjunction with Edmund Waller, marks a significant stage in the development of the heroic couplet. He included among his friends the philosopher Thomas Hobbes.

In May 1639 he joined a military campaign on the Scottish border under the royalist commander Sir Ralph Hopton. Two years later he was one of only five Cornish members to vote against the act of attainder against the Earl of Strafford, one of the King's most faithful ministers. At the end of the year 1641 he opposed the strategy of John Pym, critic of the King and leader of the Long Parliament, to control the Lords, declaring that if it was implemented 'then the Myner part of the Commons would joyne with the Major part of the Lords and enter into a protestation against them that did'. Although ordered to withdraw from the Commons until the house had time to consider his behaviour, he was one of the last royalist members to leave the house. As he went, he warned the other members that 'when the cards are shuffled, no man knows what the game will be'.

On the declaration of civil war he was an active commissioner of array, charged by King Charles I with mustering royalist troops in the south-west. In September 1642 he accompanied Hopton on a march through north Devon and into Cornwall. As a member of Hopton's council of war he fought with the army at the battle of Braddock Down in January 1643, a royalist victory, and took part in the subsequent advance that drove the Parliamentarian army across the Tamar into Devon.

Three weeks later he was among a party of volunteers led by Sir John Berkeley setting out from Plympton in pursuit of the Parliamentary forces. On 8 February, while heading from Okehampton towards Totnes, the force was ambushed at Chagford by an army under the command of Sir John Northcott. Godolphin was riding through the town when he was shot above the knee, and he fell dead from his horse. He was thought to have married shortly before his death, leaving a daughter, though neither his wife not child were referred to in his will. He was buried at Okehampton church on 10 February 1643.

Sidney Godolphin

Government Minister

Sidney Godolpin was born in Godolphin Hall near Helston on 15 June 1645. He was appointed page of honour to King Charles II in 1662, and at court became a lifelong friend of John Churchill, later Duke of Marlborough, a political ally and then page to the Duke of York, heir to the throne and later King James II. In 1668 he was elected MP for Helston. That same year he acted as an intermediary between the King and his sister Henrietta Anne, wife of the Duke of Anjou, King Louis XIV's brother, in negotiations with the French King by which Charles II would abandon his Dutch allies in return for French money. In recognition of his success he was made a groom of the bedchamber and awarded an annual pension of £500. The next year he obtained a thirty-one-year lease on all tin mines discovered in Rialton and Retraigh. In 1672 the King appointed him envoy-extraordinary to Louis XIV, in order to assure Louis of Charles's support before he took the field against the Dutch.

In 1680 he voted for the Exclusion Bill designed to remove the Catholic Duke of York from the line of succession (though it was never passed as the King dissolved Parliament), and was created Baron Godolphin of Rialton in 1684. After the accession of the Duke as James II he was chamberlain to Queen Mary, and in 1687 he was named commissioner of the treasury. As one of the King's most trusted confidantes, he was one of the council of five appointed by James to represent him in London when he went to join the army after William of Orange landed in England in 1688. Godolphin, Halifax and Nottingham were sent to negotiate with the Prince. When Godolphin returned to London, James had fled, and he argued to retain James as King but with his powers carried out by a Regency, but Parliament argued that James had abdicated the throne and offered it to the

Prince and Princess of Orange who subsequently became King William III and Queen Mary II. The new King reinstated Godolphin as Commissioner to the Treasury in 1690 because of his outstanding political and economic skills, though Godolphin and the Duke of Marlborough still maintained a secret correspondence with James II. During his period of office the Bank of England was created in 1694.

After the discovery of an attempted assassination plot against William III in 1696 Godolphin, who was compromised, resigned his office, but was reappointed 1st Commissioner of the Treasury in 1700, and again after Queen Anne's accession in 1702. Godolphin, Marlborough, and Robert Harley, later 1st Earl of Oxford, became the Queen's senior ministers. He persuaded her gradually to eject the Tories from office, and with Marlborough he helped bring about union with Scotland in 1707. Knighted in 1704, and created Viscount Rialton and Earl of Godolphin in 1706, he fell from favour with the Queen after a breach with Harley, whose resignation was forced by Marlborough and Godolphin in 1708 when they threatened a mass resignation of cabinet members. As lord treasurer, Godolphin gave financial support for Marlborough's military campaigns during the War of the Spanish Succession from 1701 onwards, but had to seek Whig support to remain in office and continue the increasingly unpopular conflict. The Queen dismissed him in 1710.

A devotee of horse racing, cards and cockfighting, he was among the first to import Arab stallions into England and thus improve English racehorses; all throughbreds in English racing today can trace their bloodline back to his stable. He died on 15 September 1712.

William Golding

Author

William Gerald Golding was born in St Columb Minor on 19 September 1911, son of Alec Golding, a schoolmaster. He studied natural sciences and then English at Brasenose College, Oxford, where he was awarded a BA in English and a diploma in education. Having begun writing when he was seven, he published his first book, *A Collection of Poems*, in 1934.

He began his teaching career in 1935, initially at Streatham, before taking up similar posts in Maidstone and then Salisbury, where he taught English and philosophy at Bishop Wordsworth's School. He married Ann Brookfield in 1939 and for several years they lived in Wiltshire. During the First World War he served on HMS *Galatea* in the North Atlantic, was involved in the sinking of the German battleship *Bismarck* in 1940, and then went to Liverpool to work on guard duty in the Gladstone Dock. In the spring of 1942 he was seconded to MD1, a weapons research unit in Buckinghamshire. The following year he returned to sea, and was sent to New York to help bring minesweepers back to Britain after they had been built in the New Jersey dockyards. Later he was trained in landing crafts equipped with rocket guns, and while commanding these he took part in the naval support for the D-Day landings and the invasion of Walcheren.

Demobilised in 1945, he returned to writing and teaching. His experiences during the war were a major influence on his writing, and he remarked that 'man produces evil, as a bee produces honey.' Originally called *Strangers from Within*, his first novel *Lord of the Flies* was rejected by twenty-one publishers before it appeared in 1954. This story about a group of children evacuated from Britain during nuclear war to an uninhabited island always remained his most successful work, being translated into several languages and filmed twice. It was followed by eleven more novels, including *The Inheritors* (1955), *Pincher Martin* (1956), *Free Fall* (1959), *The Spire* (1964), and *The Paper Men* (1984). During his writing career he published twelve novels as well as short stories, plays, essays and reviews.

In 1961 he spent the academic year at Hollins College, Virginia, USA, then resigned his teaching post at Bishop Wordsworth's School to concentrate on writing full-time. He was made an honorary fellow of Brasenose College, Oxford, awarded the CBE in 1966, and an honorary D.Litt was conferred on him by the University of Sussex in 1968.

He was awarded the Booker Prize for Literature in 1980 for *Rites Of Passage*, the first volume of the trilogy *To the Ends of the Earth*, portraying life aboard an ancient ship of the line during the Napoleonic Wars. It was concluded in *Close Quarters* (1987) and *Fire Down Below* (1989). In 1983 he was awarded the Nobel Prize for Literature, the Nobel Foundation citing 'his novels which, with the perspicuity of realistic narrative art and the diversity and universality of myth, illuminate the human condition in the world of today'.

In 1985 Golding and his wife moved to Tullimaar, in Perranarworthal, a large Regency house six miles from Truro, surrounded by woods and gardens. That same year he published a travel memoir, *An Egyptian Journal*. He died at his home on 19 June 1993 [see D.M. Thomas]. His last novel, *The Double Tongue*, set in ancient Greece, was left in draft form at his death and published in 1995.

Winston Graham

Author

Winston Mawdsley Graham was born in Manchester, son of Albert Graham, tea importer, and his wife Anne. According to his death certificate he was born on 30 June 1908, while other sources give the year as 1910. 'In *Who's Who* I don't give my birth date,' he wrote later, 'and in four other similar publications around the world I have given different dates, all of them wrong.' He dictated his first story to his mother when he was five. It had been planned that he would go to Manchester Grammar School until he contracted meningitis at the age of seven. Because of persistent ill-health he went instead to Longsight Grammar School. After his father had a stroke the family moved to Perranporth, and Cornwall provided the setting and inspiration for much of his writing.

His first published novel, *The House with the Stained Glass Windows* (1934), a murder mystery, earned him a mere £29. During the Second World War he served with the auxiliary coastguard service, while continuing to publish novels including *Night Journey* (1941) and *The Merciless Lady* (1944), both of which he later revised.

Several of his suspense novels were filmed, including *The Forgotten Story* (1945), *Marnie* (1961), *Fortune is a Woman* (1953), *The Sleeping Partner* (1956), and *The Walking Stick* (1967). He won the first Golden Dagger award of the Crime Writers' Association in 1955. While writing a boxing novel, *Angell, Pearl And Little God* (1970), he met boxer Henry Cooper and promoter Mike Barrett, and sat in the front row of a boxing match at the Albert Hall.

However his reputation rests largely on the twelve Poldark novels, each subtitled 'a novel of Cornwall'. The first, *Ross Poldark: a Novel of Cornwall, 1783–1787* (1945), was followed a year later by *Demelza*, the tale of Ross's wife. *Jeremy Poldark* (1950), and *Warleggan* (1953) brought the story up to 1793. Convinced they were less successful than his suspense novels, he decided at one stage not to write any more in the series. Nevertheless a fifth, *The Black Moon*, which took the Poldark saga into the nineteenth century, followed in 1973. Two years later the chronicle was dramatised by BBC TV, with a further series following in 1977. It regularly attracted up to 15 million viewers, and throughout Cornwall churches altered the times of their services to avoid clashing with transmission. More Poldark novels followed, and while writing the last, *Bella Poldark* (2002), in which the heroine goes to London and becomes an opera singer, for his research he persuaded English National Opera to let him see a rehearsal of Rossini's *The Barber of Seville*.

His literary career spanned more than seventy years and forty-six books which made him, in his own words, 'the most successful unknown novelist in England', and he called his autobiography *Memoirs of a Private Man* (2003). Reluctant to court publicity, he believed a writer should appear on the printed page rather than the public stage. Even at the height of Poldark's popularity he seldom gave interviews. For a while he lived in France and paid tax in Switzerland but returned home as, he said, he would rather be taxed to death than bored to death. He was chairman of the Society of Authors from 1967 to 1969 and a fellow of the Royal Society of Literature. In 1983 he was awarded the OBE. He died on 10 July 2003 at Abbotswood House Nursing Home, Buxted, East Sussex.

Geoffrey Grigson

Author

Geoffrey Edward Harvey Grigson was born on 2 March 1905 at Pelynt, the seventh and youngest son of Canon William Shuckforth Grigson, vicar of Pelynt, and his wife Mary. As a boy he enjoyed studying and exploring the local archaeology, topography and natural history, climbing trees to collect birds' eggs, and fishing. He was educated at Leatherhead and St Edmund Hall, Oxford, where he gained a third class in English in 1927.

He first became well known in the 1930s as a poet. In 1933 he was appointed editor of the poetry magazine *New Verse*, marking the start of a versatile literary career which would embrace not only verse but also verse and prose anthologies, art criticism, memoirs, and guides to the countryside. At various times he was involved in teaching, journalism and broadcasting. During the First World War he worked in the editorial department of the BBC Monitoring Service at Wood Norton near Evesham.

Afterwards he became a full-time freelance writer, making his home in a farmhouse near Swindon. He had a lifelong interest in English Romantic art, publishing a volume of essays on the subject, *The Harp of Aeolus* (1947). A biography, *Samuel Palmer: the Visionary Years* (1947), did much to restore the then largely forgotten painter's reputation. His anthologies included *The Romantics* (1943), *Before the Romantics* (1946), and *The Faber Book of Popular Verse* (1971). *The Crest on the Silver* (1950) was an autobiography, and *Freedom of the Parish* (1954), while part memoir, is also regarded as one of the modern classics about Cornish churches and the local countryside. His other titles on similar subjects included *The Englishman's Flora* (1955), *The Shell Country Book* (1962), and *Britain Observed: The Landscape Through Artists' Eyes* (1975). He edited *The Concise Encyclopedia of Modern World Literature* (1970), and as a critic, he contributed reviews to journals including *The Times Literary Supplement* and *New York Review of Books*.

He published thirteen collections of poetry, making his aims clear in the first, *Several Observations* (1939), of 'taking notice, for ends not purely individual, of the universe of objects and events'. His *Collected Poems 1924-62* appeared in 1963, and a further volume covering the years 1963 to 1980 in 1982. That same year he published *The Private Art*, a 'poetry notebook' of comments and quotations.

He distrusted all official bodies dealing with the arts, and refused to serve on any committees. In 1972 he received the Duff Cooper memorial prize for a volume of poems, but his short acceptance speech at the ceremony showed how uncomfortable he was with appearing at such functions.

His first wife, Frances Galt, whom he married in 1929, died of tuberculosis in 1937. A second marriage to Berta Kunert in 1938 ended in divorce, and he married Jane McIntire, who as Jane Grigson later became a well-known cookery writer, as did their daughter Sophie. He said she 'ruined my figure, and saved my soul'. He died on 28 November 1985 at their Swindon home, and was buried in the nearby churchyard at Broad Town. A final collection of verse, *Persephone's Flowers*, was published in 1986.

Sir Goldsworthy Gurney

Inventor

Goldsworthy Gurney was born in Avon Cottage, Treator, near Padstow, on 14 February 1793. His Christian name was taken from his godmother, a maid of honour to Queen Charlotte. He was educated at Truro, where he excelled at contemporary sciences and met Richard Trevithick. After studying medicine he settled at Wadebridge in 1814 practising as a surgeon, while continuing to pursue his interests in chemistry and mechanical science. That same year he married Elizabeth Symons.

In 1820 the family moved to Argyle Street, near Hanover Square, London, where he continued his medical practice and lectured on the elements of chemical science to the Surrey Institution, where he was appointed lecturer in 1822.

By 1823 he had given up medicine, to spend more time experimenting with the construction of steam engines, particularly the idea of a vehicle propelled by steam to provide road travel. In 1825 he started working on a steam carriage in a small workshop in Oxford Street and filing a first patent for 'An apparatus for propelling carriages on common roads or railways without the aid of horses, with sufficient speed for the carriage of passengers and goods'. He was also involved with the development of the blastpipe, which used steam to increase the flow of air through a steam engine's chimney, thus increasing the draw of air over the fire and much increasing the power to weight ratio of a steam engine. In 1826 he moved to Albany Street and took over the premises of an American inventor and engineer, Jacob Perkins, who was working on the construction of a 'steam gun'. In 1829 one of his steam coaches went from London to Bath and back at 15mph.

In 1823 he was awarded an Isis gold medal of the Royal Society of Arts for devising an oxy-hydrogen blowpipe, in which an intense flame was created by burning a jet of oxygen and hydrogen together. He also devised improved lighting systems, by using a standard oil lamp to produce a flame, and then introduced oxygen gas into the middle of the flame. The unburned carbon in the oil flame burned very brightly and an intense white light was produced from the weak yellow flame of the oil lamp. This system was fitted in the House of Commons and Trafalgar Square. He also invented a better form of lighting for lighthouses, realising if each lighthouse had a different flashing system, sailors could know which one they were looking at. In 1854 he was appointed superintendent of the heating, lighting and ventilating systems at the Houses of Parliament.

In 1830 he leased a plot of land overlooking Summerleaze Beach, Bude, and began the construction of a new house in the sand hills. After his wife died in 1837 his daughter Mary Anne became his constant companion, and they moved to Reeds, a small house at Ploughill, near Bude. In 1844 he bought a lease on Hornacott Manor, Boyton, ten miles from Bude, where he built Woodleigh Cottage for himself, and engaged his interest in farming. He still divided his time between London and Cornwall, continuing to experiment with heating (the Gurney Stove, patented in 1856, was extensively used to heat buildings) and electrical conduction, and was appointed president of the Launceston Agricultural Society.

In 1863 he was knighted. Later that year he had a paralytic stroke, sold Hornacott and retired to Reeds, where he died apparently penniless on 28 February 1875 and was buried at Launcells Church near Bude.

William Hals

Antiquary

William Hals was born in 1654 at Tresawen, Merther, the second son of James Hals of Fentongollan and Anne, daughter and co-heir of John Martin of Hurston, Devon. His father served at the siege of La Rochelle in 1628, and later in the West Indies.

According to his son, he was appointed governor of Montserrat. He held Tresawen by lease from his mother.

Few details of Hals's life are known, and he is remembered mainly for the scholarship and studies he left behind him. Among the surviving manuscripts he left are a translation of Keigwin's *Mount Calvary*. He began researching a history of Cornwall at about the age of thirty, an interest which occupied him for the rest of his life. He left a manuscript of *the Parochial history of Cornwall* which had the appearance of a working copy and, although described as nearly completed at his death, was probably never intended for publication in its existing form. He was thrice married, his first two wives belonging respectively to the families of Evans of Landrinis in Wales and Carveth of Pewansand. In 1714 he married Jane Courtney of Tremeer; they had no children, and his wife died some time before 1736. He died around 1737 at Tregury, St Wenn.

His manuscripts passed to his kinsman William Halse of Truro, who in about 1750 arranged for the *Compleat History of Cornwall* to be published by Andrew Brice of Exeter in weekly sixpenny numbers of four sheets, a financial rather than a scholarly venture. The publishers began with the second part of the work, a parochial history taken directly from the manuscript. Hals had also written *History of St Michael's Mount* and *Dictionary of the Cornish Language*, which were intended as part of the final work. It seems that the venture proved unsuccessful and only seventy-two parishes (Advent to Helston) appeared. The suspension of the work was said to have been due to the scurrilous anecdotes it contained, although Lysons blamed the inaccuracies and 'tedious' legends of saints. In style is was very similar to the county histories of the early seventeenth century, in which Cornwall was amply represented by Richard Carew's *Survey of Cornwall*. Hals's manuscript was later incorporated into the nineteenth-century parochial histories of Cornwall produced by Davies Gilbert (q.v.) and Joshua Polsue.

John Harris

Poet

John Harris was born on 14 October 1820 at Six Chimneys Cottage, Bolenowe Hill, near Camborne, the eldest of ten children. His father was a miner at Dolcoath tin mine and John also went to work down the mines at the age of about ten. He had been writing poetry since he was a child, usually in the open air where he was inspired by nature. Much of his work celebrated the scenery of the countryside and coast around him, especially around Carn Brea and the scenic splendours of Land's End and the Lizard. As he was unable to afford ink or paper, he wrote in blackberry juice on grocery wrapping paper. Sometimes he recited his work to the other miners. One piece, a dirge on the death of some men killed in Carn Brea mine, was printed, and sung by a blind man in the streets of Camborne. Several friends, including Hugh Rogers, rector of Camborne, encouraged him by lending him books which gave him a wider knowledge of English poetry.

In 1845 he married Jane Rule, and they had two sons and two daughters. The death of their second daughter, Lucretia, from pneumonia at Christmas 1855, inspired an eulogy in verse.

After he had been down the mines for twenty years, one of his poems was published in a magazine, and attracted some attention. His first collection of poems, *Lays from the Mine, the Moor, and the Mountain*, was printed by subscription with the help of George Smith, in 1853, and a second edition appeared in 1856. In August 1857 he obtained a small appointment as scripture reader in Falmouth, and he gave up his work at the mines. For some years he had been a local preacher among the Wesleyans, and a Sunday school teacher since he was sixteen. From time to time he contributed to religious periodicals and tract society publications.

In 1864 he entered a poetry competition celebrating the tercentenary of Shakespeare's birth, and won the first prize which enabled him to visit Stratford-upon-Avon, the only journey he ever made away from Cornwall throughout his life. He received grants from the Royal Literary Fund in 1872 and 1875, while Lord Beaconsfield and Gladstone each secured him £200 from the Royal Bounty Fund. He published several volumes of poetry and essays during his lifetime, including *A Story of Carn Brea*, which he described as the pagan mountain of his childhood, *The Land's End, Kynance Cove*, and other poems, and *Linto and Laneer*. His best remembered poem today is probably 'The Cornish Chough', dedicated to the traditional symbol of Cornwall.

In April 1878 he was struck with paralysis, and confined to his room for two months. Four years later he published his *Autobiography*. At the end of 1883 a fall led to spasmodic asthma attacks. He died at his home, Killigrew Terrace, Falmouth, on 7 January 1884 and in accordance with his wishes he was buried at Treslothan, Cornwall, on 10 January. A biography, *John Harris, the Cornish Poet* by his son James, writing as John Howard, was published later that year. His poetry remained out of print for a long time, but a resurgence of interest in his work followed another biography by Paul Newman, *The Meads of Love* (1994).

Robert Stephen Hawker

Poet and Clergyman

Robert Stephen Hawker was born on 3 December 1803 at the vicarage of Charles Church, Plymouth, the eldest of ten children, son of Jacob Stephen Hawker, MD, vicar of Stratton. Educated at Liskeard and Cheltenham Grammar Schools, he was reading and writing poetry by the age of ten. At sixteen he was placed with a solicitor at Plymouth, but found the law 'distasteful' to him. Three years later he married his godmother, Charlotte I'ans, aged forty-one. They spent their honeymoon at Tintagel, a place which kindled Hawker's lifelong fascination with Arthurian legend. This marriage and a legacy helped to finance his studies at Pembroke College, Oxford, where he won the Newdigate Prize for poetry in 1827. Taking Anglican orders in 1831, he became curate at North Tamerton and then vicar of Morwenstow, noted for its numerous smugglers and wreckers, where he stayed the rest of his life. He was the first vicar in residence there for over a century.

He became known for giving Christian burials to shipwrecked seamen washed up on the shores of the parish. Previously such sailors had been buried on the beach where they were found or left to the sea. At the entrance to Morwenstow Churchyard stands

the figurehead of the ship *Caledonia* which foundered in September 1842, marking the grave of nine of the ten-man crew. Nearby is a granite cross marked 'Unknown Yet Well Known', marking the mass grave of about thirty seafarers, including the captain of the *Alonzo*, also wrecked in 1842. He introduced the Harvest Festival in Morwenstow in 1843 by inviting his parishioners to a Harvest service, at which he wanted to give thanks to God for providing such plenty in a fitting way. It took place on 1 October with bread made from the first cut of corn taken at communion.

His first volume of poems, *Tendrils*, was published in 1821. As a poet, he was best remembered for Cornwall's unofficial national anthem, 'The Song of the Western Men', including the line 'And shall Trelawney die? There's 20,000 Cornish men shall know the reason why', which he published anonymously in 1825. His name became known after Charles Dickens acknowledged his authorship of the song in the serial magazine *Household Words*.

'Parson Hawker', as he was known to his parishioners, was a genuine eccentric, in his clothes and his habits, loving bright colours, the only black garments he wore being his socks. He wore a claret-coloured coat, or a blue fisherman's jersey, long sea-boots, a pink brimless hat and a poncho made from a yellow horse blanket, which he claimed was the ancient habit of St Pardarn, walked his pet pig, talked to birds, invited his nine cats into church, and once excommunicated one for catching mice on Sundays. The vicarage he built himself had chimneys modelled on the towers of the churches in his life, Tamerton, where he had been curate; Morwenstow and Wellcombe; and that of Magdalen College, Oxford. The kitchen chimney was a replica of his mother's tomb. 'Hawker's Hut', which he built from driftwood on the cliffs overlooking the Atlantic Ocean, and where he spent hours writing poetry, is currently the smallest property owned by the National Trust.

His wife died in 1863 and the next year he married Pauline Kuczynski, aged twenty; they had three daughters. He died on 15 August 1875, after having converted to the Roman Catholic Church on his deathbed, and was buried in Ford Park cemetery, Plymouth. By his request, at his funeral the mourners wore purple instead of black.

Dame Barbara Hepworth

Sculptor

Jocelyn Barbara Hepworth was born on 10 January 1903 at Wakefield, Yorkshire, eldest of four children of Herbert Raikes Hepworth, a civil engineer, and his wife, Gertrude Allison Johnson. She studied at Leeds School of Art and the Royal College of Art, London. A fellow student at both was Henry Moore, who remained a friend and colleague for the whole of her working life. On completing her course at the Royal College she was awarded the diploma of associateship in July 1923, returned for a year as a postgraduate and was short-listed for the prix de Rome in sculpture. Though she did not win the award, her work was commended and she was awarded a scholarship for a year's travel abroad. While visiting Rome in November 1924 she met John Skeaping, another sculptor, and they were married in Florence in May 1925. During the year they spent there she learned how to carve stone. Returning to London they settled in St John's Wood, and then in Hampstead. In June 1928 they had their first major exhibition at the Beaux Arts Gallery in London, featuring mostly stone carvings of figures and animals. It was followed by a second at the gallery of Arthur Tooth & Son, London, in October 1930.

In 1931 she met the painter Ben Nicholson, and they lived together from the following year. Her marriage to Skeaping was dissolved in 1933. In 1931–2 she had made a small near-abstract sculpture, *Pierced Form*, in alabaster, destroyed in the Second World War, of which the dominant feature was a large hole in the centre. It was shown at Tooth's Gallery in November 1932, at a joint exhibition also featuring the work of Nicholson. Another joint exhibition was staged in October 1933 at the Lefevre Gallery, where she showed her work regularly for the next twenty years.

By this time she was producing what was regarded as among the first completely abstract sculptures, initially very simple abstract shapes with titles such as Single Form, Two Forms, and Pierced Hemisphere. Regular visits to Paris between 1933 and 1935 had put her and Nicolson in personal contact with artists including Braque, Picasso, Brancusi, Arp, Miró, and Mondrian. By the end of the 1930s their studio in Parkhill Road was the centre of the abstract art movement in Britain, and other leading names such as Henry and Irina Moore, and Herbert Read, the poet and art writer, lived nearby.

Hepworth and Nicolson were married in 1938, and on the outbreak of war they and their triplet children left London for St Ives. In 1942 they moved into a house at Headland Road, in the Carbis Bay suburb of St Ives, and after a break of a few years, in 1943 she took up sculpture again. Her new work reflected a strongly Cornish influence, with references to local landscape forms, the patterns of nature, the movement of tides, pebble and rock formations, and the Cornish moorland landscape.

In 1949 she purchased Trewyn Studio, St Ives, where she lived from 1950. It provided her with a garden in which to work and display her sculptures, as well as living and working accommodation on two floors. Around this time she was invited to undertake various commissions, including two for the Festival of Britain in 1951 (the year she and Nicolson divorced), and one apiece for the office block State House, High Holborn, and for the John Lewis Partnership for their flagship Oxford Street store. By the time she was made a CBE in 1958 and DBE in 1965, she was regarded as the world's greatest woman sculptor. In her last years she suffered from throat cancer, and she died in a fire at her studio on 20 May 1975.

Antony Hewish

Astronomer and Nobel Prize Winner

Antony Hewish was born in Fowey on 11 May 1924, the youngest of three sons of a banker. He grew up in Newquay and during childhood he developed a love of the sea and boats. Educated at King's College, Taunton, he went on to study for an undergraduate degree at Gonville and Caius College, Cambridge, which was interrupted by war service. Between 1943 and 1946 he worked at the Royal Aircraft Establishment, Farnborough and the Telecommunications Research Establishment, Malvern.

On his return to Cambridge in 1946, he completed his degree and joined fellow radio astronomer Martin Ryle's research team at the Cavendish Laboratory, working on airborne radar-counter-measure devices, and obtaining his Ph.D. in 1952. He became a research fellow at Gonville and Caius College, and in 1961 transferred to Churchill College as director of studies in physics. During his time as university lecturer, a post he held from 1961 to 1969, he undertook extensive research in radio astronomy. His decision to do so was influenced partly by his wartime experience with electronics and antennas and partly by his teacher, Jack Ratcliffe, head of radiophysics at the Cavendish Laboratory, who inspired him with a course on electromagnetic theory during his final undergraduate year. He made practical and theoretical advances in the observation and exploitation of the apparent scintillations, or 'twinkling', of radio sources due to their radiation impinging upon plasma, and realised that such activity could be used to probe conditions in the ionosphere.

In 1965 he proposed and secured funding for, the construction of the Interplanetary Scintillation Array, a large array radio telescope at the Mullard Radio Astronomy Observatory, Cambridge, so he could conduct a high time-resolution radio survey of interstellar scintillation. It was completed in 1967, and during construction one of his graduate students, Jocelyn Bell, first noticed the radio source which was ultimately recognised as the first pulsar.

He was university reader from 1969 to 1971 and Professor of Radio Astronomy from 1971 until his retirement in 1989. In 1968 he was made a Fellow of the Royal Society, and in 1969 he was awarded the Eddington Medal of the Royal Astronomical Society. Five years later he and Ryle were jointly awarded the Nobel Prize for Physics for their work on the development of radio aperture synthesis and its role in the discovery of pulsars. After Ryle had to retire as a result of ill-health in 1977 he assumed leadership of the Cambridge radio astronomy group, and was head of the Mullard Radio Astronomy Observatory from 1982 to 1988.

As well as lecturing at the university, he worked for some years with the Royal Institution, London when it was directed by Sir Lawrence Bragg, giving one of the Christmas Lectures and subsequently several Friday Evening Discourses. It has always been his belief that 'scientists have a duty to share the excitement and pleasure of their work with the general public', and he enjoys 'the challenge of presenting difficult ideas in an understandable way'.

Emily Hobhouse

Humanitarian Worker

Emily Hobhouse was born in Liskeard on 9 April 1860, daughter of the Revd Reginald Hobhouse and Caroline Trelawny, and educated at home. In 1895 she went to Minnesota to carry out welfare work amongst Cornish mineworkers there. She became engaged to John Carr Jackson and they bought a ranch in Mexico, but the engagement was broken off and she returned home in 1898, having lost most of her money in a speculative venture.

Strongly opposed to the Boer War, she addressed several public meetings during the first few weeks of fighting, attacking the government's course of action. When she learned of the British army's ill-treatment of women and children, she was determined to go to South Africa and help them, and in October 1900 she formed the Relief Fund for South African Women and Children to feed, clothe, and save those left destitute through destruction of property or eviction. Arriving in South Africa on 27 December, she was grudgingly granted permission to visit the British army's concentration camps. When Lord Kitchener objected, she was only allowed to see Bloemfontein, where she arrived in January 1901 to discover inadequate basic provision and accommodation for the 1,800 people there. When she complained about the lack of soap she was told it was a luxury, but managed to have it recategorised as a necessity, as well as straw and kettles for boiling drinking water. Over the next few weeks she visited several camps and everywhere she brought to the authorities' attention the inadequate sanitary accommodation and inadequate rations.

When she returned to England to ask the government to stop the army's scorched earth and concentration-camp policy, few members of Parliament expressed any concern. At length the ministers agreed to set up a committee of women headed by Millicent Fawcett. Hobhouse was not invited to join the committee and complained that Fawcett had already spoken in favour of British concentration camps. She decided to return to South Africa, but was warned she would not be allowed back into the camps. On trying to re-enter Cape Town in October 1901, she was forcibly transferred to another ship and deported. Back in South Africa in 1903 after peace was signed, she set up various resettlement and rehabilitation projects, including the establishment of industrial schools for lace making, spinning, and weaving, and in 1907 was appointed an adviser to manage public funds for the schools before leaving Africa for the last time in October 1908.

During the First World War, she worked at the secretariat for the international women's movement for peace in Amsterdam for three months in 1915. In 1916 she travelled through Germany and Belgium to investigate conditions for refugees, interned civilians, and prisoners of war, and in England she helped to promote schemes for the exchange of prisoners of war. She became an honorary citizen for her humanitarian work in South Africa, where in 1921 a sum of £2,300 was collected from the people and sent to her in recognition of her work on their behalf during the Boer War, to buy herself a property on the Cornish coast. She purchased a house in St Ives, now part of the Porthminster Hotel, where a commemorative plaque to her was unveiled by the South African High Commissioner.

She contracted pleurisy and died in London on 8 June 1926, and on 26 October her ashes were buried at the Bloemfontein war memorial.

Leonard Hobhouse

Journalist

Leonard Trelawney Hobhouse, younger brother of Emily Hobhouse (q.v.), was born in St Ives, near Liskeard, on 8 September 1864. Under the influence of his uncle, Arthur, Lord Hobhouse, a Gladstonian Liberal, he became a committed radical and a firm agnostic while at Marlborough College. At Corpus Christi College, Oxford, his radical opinions, which endorsed home rule and the abolition of the monarchy, brought him notoriety and the presidency of the Oxford Radical Club. He graduated in 1887 with a first in classics and won a prize fellowship at Merton. In 1890 he was appointed assistant tutor at Corpus Christi and four years later was elected fellow of the college. He initially taught philosophy, specialising in epistemology, but a study of trade unionism gave him a strong interest in sociology. His first book, *The Labour Movement* (1893), was followed by *The Theory of Knowledge* (1896).

He watched with interest a campaign to unionise local agricultural labourers, and was a trustee of the Oxfordshire Agricultural Labourers Union. In 1896 he was persuaded to write for the *Manchester Guardian* by the editor, C.P. Scott; the following year he left academic life and for six years worked full-time for the paper. He and Scott remained ever critical of the Unionists, the Liberal Imperialists, and the war against the Boers. Further books followed, *Mind in Evolution* (1901), *Democracy and Reaction* (1904), and *Morals in Evolution* (1906). In 1903 he returned to academic work, as well as becoming editor of the *Sociological Review*, paid secretary and organiser of the Free Trade Union, a Liberal campaigning group, and an active member of the Adult Suffrage Society. He left the FTU in 1905 to become political editor of a new London-based Liberal-inclined newspaper, *The Tribune*. Its first issue came out in 1906, just after the party's landslide election victory, but for financial reasons moved to a more populist line under the managing editor and Hobhouse resigned within a few months. It did not long survive his departure.

In 1907 he became Professor of Sociology at the London School of Economics. He continued to contribute articles to the *Manchester Guardian* throughout the rest of his career, and in 1911 became a director of the paper. In 1909 he was offered the chance to stand as Liberal candidate for Parliament for Northampton, but declined. In 1914 he, Scott and Charles Montague, called for Britain to maintain neutrality in the growing conflict in Europe, but after the declaration of war he gave his support to the government. By 1917 he had become disillusioned by the growing number of casualties and urged a negotiated peace. After the war he published several more books, including *The Rational Good* (1921), *The Elements of Social Justice* (1922) and *Social Development* (1924).

Though an ardent trade union supporter, he never joined the Labour party as he took issue with the principle of a political party based on sectional interest. Nevertheless in his later years he advocated a progressive alliance between the Liberals and Labour while the latter were gradually replacing the former as an alternative party of government to the Conservatives.

As his health declined, he spent part of each summer in Bagnôles de l'Orne in Normandy on medical advice. He died in hospital in Alençon, France, on 21 June 1929 after suffering from a duodenal ulcer, and was buried in Wimbledon.

Silas Hocking

Novelist and United Methodist Minister

Silas Kitto Hocking was born at St Stephen, Brannel, on 24 March 1850, third son of James Hocking, part owner of a tin mine, and his wife Elizabeth. Educated at local grammar schools and later privately, in 1869 he was accepted as a candidate for the ministry of the United Methodist Free Churches, and was ordained in 1870. He held pastorates at Pontypool, Spalding, Liverpool, and Manchester. While working in Liverpool he married Esther Mary Lloyd in 1876, and they had one son and two daughters. His first novel, *Alec Green*, was published in 1878 and sold moderately well, but was eclipsed the following year by *Her Benny*, a story of street children in Liverpool, the copyright of which he sold for £20. It sold over a million copies, and was translated into several languages.

In 1879 he was made a fellow of the Royal Historical Society. Four years later he settled in Southport, where during the next thirteen years he preached to crowded congregations. In 1884 he undertook a lecture tour of Canada in association with the British Association of Methodist Churches. In 1894 he became editor of the *Family Circle*, and two years later he and Frederick Anthony Atkins established the T*emple Magazine*, a sixpenny illustrated monthly journal for Sunday reading.

He resigned from the ministry in 1896 in order to devote himself to writing, lecturing, and journalism. An interest in Liberal politics led to him unsuccessfully contesting the seat of Aylesbury in the 1906 general election and Coventry in that of January 1910. Altogether he wrote over fifty books, and at one time was said to be not only the best-selling English novelist of the time, but also the first author to sell a million books in his lifetime. His most popular titles, many of which were didactic in nature, included *For Light and Liberty* (1890), *Where Duty Lies* (1891), *A Son of Reuben* (1894), *For Such is Life* (1896), *In Spite of Fate* (1897), *Gripped* (1902) and *Who Shall Judge* (1910). He also published an autobiography, *My Book of Memory* (1923).

He was regarded as one of the last of the 'Evangelical books for children' authors, and his titles were regarded as being largely concerned with leading children to religion. They soon went out of fashion, and he has remained largely unknown to later generations. He died at his home in Highgate, Middlesex, on 15 September 1935.

His brother Joseph was also born at St Stephen, on 7 November 1860, entered the ministry of the United Methodist Free Churches in 1880, and was ordained four years later. Like Silas he spent part of his career in the church, and was also a prolific author, publishing fifty-three titles altogether. He was minister of Woodford Green Church, Essex, until resigning in 1910. Some of his titles, notably *The Romance of Michael Trevail* (1909) and *Felicity Trevenbyn* (1928), are set in Cornwall, though most of the others, among them *Jabez Easterbrook* (1891), and *The Trampled Cross* (1907), have a strong religious tone. He died at Perranporth on 4 March 1937.

Al Hodge

Guitarist

Alan ('Big Al') Hodge was born in Bodmin in 1951. At first he wanted to be a painter and decorator, but when he was twelve his father bought him a guitar and amplifier, 'and I was so happy I cried'. He joined The Jaguars as rhythm (later lead) guitarist while still at school. At the age of sixteen he turned professional with The Onyx, who played gigs throughout Britain, released seven singles, none of which ever made the charts, and recorded several sessions for broadcast on BBC Radio 1.

In 1970 he returned to Cornwall and joined a Bodmin group, Ginhouse. In the following year he joined the Sawmills Studio, Golant, near Fowey, as a session guitarist, which led to his playing on recordings by acts including Lesley Duncan, Clifford T. Ward and Splinter. In 1975 he joined songwriting duo Guy Fletcher and Doug Flett, and fellow musician John Hodkinson, to form the group Rogue, who recorded several singles and three albums during their four-year existence.

Despite making regular appearances on BBC TV's *The Two Ronnies* and other shows, they had greater success in Europe, particularly in terms of record sales, than at home.

Meanwhile, in 1978 he had formed The Mechanics, who were basically the Sawmills house session band, and also included studio manager and drummer Al Eden, and bass player Dave Quinn. They released several singles and albums, as well as teaming up with Leo Sayer as his backing band on two world tours and a six-part series for BBC TV in 1983. In America they worked with various singers including Linda Ronstadt, Vanessa Williams and Randy Crawford, and with Bill Cosby, they did sixty shows in thirty days at the Las Vegas Hilton.

After returning to Cornwall in 1985 he formed a writing partnership with American musician Michael Dan Ehmig, which included the group Workforce. Their most successful collaboration, *Rock'n'Roll Mercenaries*, was a hit in 1986 for Meat Loaf and John Parr. Further songwriting partnerships, providing material for other singers, followed during the next few years, notably *Some Kinda Love* with Tony Cox and Lesley Duncan, a hit in Japan for Rick Astley. Further session credits included work for Suzi Quatro, Sad Café and Toyah Willcox, and in 1999 he toured Britain as guitarist in Elkie Brooks' band.

In addition to playing with and for other artists, he was also much in demand as a music teacher at schools throughout the county, and as a composer for television, radio and video. Among his credits were *Music for Wisley Through the Seasons* (BBC, 1997), and *A National Heritage*, a six-part documentary on Lanhydrock House (BBC, 2003); *The Sunday Late Show*, hosted by Chris Robinson (BBC South-West Radio), *Badgers Wood*, an instrumental played daily on the *David White Show* (BBC Radio Cornwall), music to accompany the Haynes Publishing Group video shown at the 1996 Motor Show, Earls Court, and a series of training videos for the British Heart Foundation.

In 2003 he briefly reformed The Mechanics to celebrate their 25th anniversary. Soon afterwards he was diagnosed with a brain tumour, and died at Bodmin Hospital on 13 July 2006.

T.L. Horabin

Politician

Thomas Lewis Horabin was born in Merthyr Tydfil in 1896, and educated at Cardiff High School. During the First World War he served with the Cameron Highlanders, and entered business after demobilisation. He became chairman of Lacrinoid Ltd, a button manufacturer, and practised as a business consultant.

After the death of Sir Francis Acland, Liberal MP for North Cornwall, he was adopted as Liberal candidate in the resulting by-election on 13 July 1939. As a committed radical, fiercely opposed to the government's appeasement of Nazi Germany, he was endorsed by the all-party Popular Front, his nomination papers being signed by Labour members and dissident Conservatives. He was elected with an increased majority of 1,464 over his Conservative opponent. During the Second World War he moved increasingly to the left, and became an ever more bitter critic

of Churchill's administration. In October 1944 he published a Penguin Special, *Politics Made Plain*, a guide to 'what the next election will really be about'. It was strongly critical of the Conservative and National governments, and some commentators called it 'not plain but highly coloured'.

The election in July 1945 left him as one of only twelve Liberal MPs returned to Westminster, a net loss of nine seats for the party, and his increase in majority to 2,665 was regarded as a personal triumph. Although he was seen as a lukewarm supporter of his party leadership he was appointed Chief Whip, an office he resigned in March 1946, disenchanted with what he saw as the party's drift towards the right wing. In October he left the Liberal party and declared he would sit as an Independent Liberal.

His political activities were severely curtailed for a time when he was badly injured in an aircraft accident near Folkestone in January 1947. The plane was flying from London to Bordeaux when it developed engine trouble and crashed, killing six passengers and crew. He was in hospital for several weeks, spent a long time convalescing at home and abroad, and never completely recovered. During this period, in November 1947, he took the Labour whip. When his former local constituency party asked him to resign as MP, he refused to on the grounds that the Liberal party had moved away from the principles on which he had fought the last election.

Towards the end of the Parliament the North Cornwall Liberals selected Dingle Foot, who had lost his seat at Dundee in 1945, to replace him. Horabin declined an invitation to stand there as Labour candidate in the 1950 election on the grounds that he would be fighting against people who had supported him in 1945, and in any case, campaigning in a scattered rural constituency would have been too great a strain in view of his poor health. Moreover, Labour always polled badly there. He unsuccessfully contested the equally marginal seat of Exeter, which again returned a Conservative candidate, as did North Cornwall for the first time since 1924.

Thereafter he devoted himself increasingly to his business interests as Chairman of Lacrinoid. In 1952 he took legal action against BOAC, claiming damages for personal injuries sustained in the accident and loss of goods due to the company's alleged negligence, and the matter was settled out of court. He also took up painting as a hobby, and in 1953 he collaborated with Paul Wyeth on *How to Paint in Oils*. He died at his Folkestone home on 26 April 1956.

Henry Jenner

Cornish Language Reviver

Henry Jenner was born on 8 August 1848 at Union Hill, St Columb Major, eldest of six children of Henry Lascelles Jenner, curate of St Columb. He was educated at Harlow, Essex, and worked briefly as a schoolmaster. In January 1869 he became a clerk in the court of probate in London, and began studying Cornish material in the British

Museum Library. In July 1870 he was appointed an assistant in the British Museum's Department of Manuscripts. He joined the Philological Society in 1871 and read a paper on the Cornish language in March 1873. In 1875 he visited west Cornwall to research the remains of Cornish still used by some local people, and two years later he found at the British Museum a forty-one-line fragment of early Cornish verse on the back of a charter dated 1340. That same year he married Kitty Lee Rawlings.

In 1879 he collaborated with Walter de Gray Birch on *Early Drawings and Illuminations*, and was transferred to the British Museum's Department of Printed Books. In March 1883 he was elected a fellow of the Society of Antiquaries and later served on its council. He became assistant keeper in 1900, and his last major undertaking before he retired was to help reorganise the reading-room reference books in 1907.

In August 1901 the Cowethas Kelto-Kernuak (Celtic-Cornish Society) was formed, with Jenner as vice-president. In 1903 he joined the Celtic Association and was made a bard of the Breton gorsedd (bardic assembly), taking Gwaz Mikael (Servant of Michael) as his bardic name. Both the Jenners felt a great affinity for Brittany, acknowledging Breton as the language closest to Cornish. His *A Handbook of the Cornish Language* (1904), widely seen as the beginning of the Cornish revival. That year he addressed the Pan-Celtic Congress at Caernarvon on 'Cornwall: a Celtic nation', and Cornwall was granted membership of the congress.

After he retired from the British Museum in May 1909 and moved back to Hayle, he became known as the leading authority on Cornish matters. From 1916 to 1921 he was president of the Royal Cornwall Polytechnic Society, and from 1921 to 1923 president of the Royal Institution of Cornwall. In 1920 he was made an honorary MA by the University of Wales.

That same year he helped to form the first Old Cornwall Society (OCS) at St Ives and became its president. He was also founder president of the Hayle OCS in 1923 and the Federation of Old Cornwall Societies a year later. In 1927 he was appointed honorary St Petrock lecturer in Celtic studies at the University College of the South West. In August 1928 eight Cornish people were initiated as bards of the Welsh Gorsedd. They and the Jenners formed the nucleus of the modern Cornish Gorsedd, first held in September 1928 at Boscawen-Un near St Buryan, probable site of one of the ancient British Gorsedds. Jenner, who had composed the Cornish Gorsedd ceremony in 1907, was installed as first Grand Bard. His writings included scholarly articles across the whole range of Cornish themes, Celtic and Arthurian research, liturgiology, manuscript and royalist studies, and poems, songs, and hymns in various languages. In 1932 he presided over the first Celtic congress in Truro, the first to be held in Cornwall, and attended the first church service in Cornish for 250 years, at Towednack, the following year.

He died from uraemia on 8 May 1934 at Bospowes and was buried at St Uny, Lelant. Soon after his death the Jenner Medal for Cornish scholarship was founded in his memory, first conferred in 1936.

Philip Gidley King

Naval Officer and Colonial Administrator

Philip Gidley King was born at Launceston on 23 April 1758, joined the navy at the age of twelve as captain's servant, and was commissioned as a lieutenant in 1778. He served as second lieutenant on HMS *Sirius* under Arthur Phillip on an expedition to establish a convict settlement in New South Wales. Put in charge of a party of convicts and guards to create a settlement at Norfolk Island, he and his party landed in 1788 and helped clear the land, plant crops, and build accommodation. A few months later he forestalled a mutiny planned by some of the convicts who intended to take him and other officers prisoner, then escape on the next boat.

In 1790 he returned to England to report on the problems of the New South Wales settlements. He married Anna Josepha Coombe in March 1791, and they had five children. Having been appointed Lieutenant-Governor of Norfolk Island, with an annual salary of £250, he arrived there to find the population rather restive after the previous strict regime, and he set about improving conditions by encouraging settlers, drawn from ex-convicts and ex-marines, and taking action on their grievances about low wages and high prices. By 1794 the island was self-sufficient in grain, surplus swine were being sent to Sydney, and few settlers wanted to leave.

During his administration he drew up new regulations for prices, wages, hours of work, financial deals, and the employment of convicts, and encouraged construction of barracks, wharves, bridges and houses. He promoted industries including wine,

tobacco, cotton, hemp, and whaling, and encouraged the beginning of coal mining in the area, established schools to teach convict boys to become skilled tradesmen, enlisted medical help for a programme of smallpox vaccinations, was sympathetic to missionaries, strove to keep peace with the indigenous inhabitants, and encouraged the first newspaper, the *Sydney Gazette*. Exploration led to the survey of Bass Strait and Western Port, and the discovery of Port Phillip, and settlements were established at Hobart and Port Dalrymple in Van Diemen's Land.

Unfortunately his benign rule soon made enemies. In February 1794 members of the New South Wales Corps on Norfolk Island alleged that he punished them too severely and let ex-convicts off too leniently. He sent twenty of the ringleaders to Sydney to be court-martialled, but the governor, Francis Grose, objected to King's actions and issued orders giving the military powers illegal authority over the civilian population. Though Grose later apologised, conflict with the military continued to plague the King and he returned to England in October 1796, suffering from gout. After convalescing he was appointed Governor of New South Wales with effect from September 1800. He attacked the misconduct of officers of the New South Wales Corps for illicit liquor trading, tried to discourage its importation, and began to construct a brewery. When he faced further insubordination from the New South Wales Corps, and sent an accused officer back to face a court-martial, he received little support from the authorities in England.

Though Sydney was a convict colony, he believed that ex-convicts should not be permanently disgraced; he gave opportunities to emancipists, whom he appointed to positions of responsibility, and regulated the position of assigned servants. While he directly profited from commercial deals, cattle sales, and land grants, he was modest in his dealings compared with most of his subordinates. Nevertheless growing animosity between King and the New South Wales Corps led to his resignation in 1806 and he returned to England in failing health. He settled at Tooting where he died on 3 September 1808.

Richard and John Lander

Explorers

Richard Lander (pictured) was born in 1804 and his brother John in 1807, both at the Fighting Cocks Inn, later the Dolphin Inn, Truro, where their father was the landlord.

Richard walked to London at the age of nine, and two years later sailed on a merchant ship to the West Indies, returning to England in 1818. He then lived as a servant in the homes of various wealthy families. In 1823 he went to the Cape of Good Hope in South Africa and returned home in 1824. A year later he accompanied Lt Hugh Clapperton to West Africa on an expedition down the Niger River. Their companions soon succumbed to fever, and Clapperton himself died in April 1827 near Sokoto, now part of Nigeria, leaving Richard Lander as the only surviving European member of the expedition. African tribesmen accused him of witchcraft and forced him to drink poison, but as he survived they decided that he could not possibly be a witch. He returned to England in July 1828, leaving published accounts of his travels in *Journal of Richard Lander from Kano to the Sea Coast* (1829) and *Records of Captain Clapperton's Last Expedition to Africa, with the Subsequent Adventures of the Author* (1830).

The British government sent Richard and John to explore more of the lower Niger. They landed at Badagri in March 1830 and followed the lower Niger River from Bussa to the sea. After exploring about 100 miles of the Niger River upstream, they returned to explore the Benue River and Niger Delta and found the source, route and mouths of the river Niger River, until then unmapped. In doing so they became the first Europeans to follow the course of the Niger River to its delta. They returned to Britain in 1831 and published their results in a *Journal of an Expedition to Explore the Course and Termination of the Niger* in 1832. Richard named an island in the river Niger Truro, and a hill on its bank Cornwall Mountain. In 1832 he became the first winner of the Royal Geographical Society Founder's Gold Medal, 'for important services in determining the course and termination of the Niger'.

In 1832 Richard returned to Africa as leader of an expedition organised by Macgregor Laird and other Liverpudlian merchants, planning to found a trading settlement at the junction of the Niger and Benue rivers. The expedition encountered difficulties, many personnel died from fever and the survivors failed to reach Bussa. While journeying up the river Niger in a canoe, Lander was attacked by African tribesmen and wounded by a musket ball in his thigh. He returned to the coast, but the wound became gangrenous and he died at Fernando Po on 6 February 1834. In Truro, a monument to his memory by Cornish sculptor Neville Northey Burnard was placed at the top of Lemon Street and a local secondary school was named after him. The Africans called him *Nasarah Curramaee*, meaning 'Little Christian'.

After returning to England John, who had learned the printing trade as a young man, later worked in a London customs house. He died on 6 November 1839 of a disease contracted in Africa.

Peter Lanyon

Painter

George Peter Lanyon was born in St Ives on 8 February 1918, only son of W.H. Lanyon, amateur photographer and musician. He was educated at St Erbyn's School, Penzance, and Clifton College, and studied at the Penzance School of Art. In 1938 he went to study at the Euston Road School under Victor Pasmore. The following year he met Ben Nicholson, Barbara Hepworth (q.v.) and Naum Gabo, who had all moved to St Ives on the outbreak of war, and received private art tuition from Nicholson. He came strongly under their influence, and worked in an increasingly abstract style.

During the war he was in the RAF as a flight mechanic, and between 1940 and 1945 he served in the Western Desert, Palestine and Italy. In 1946 he married Sheila St John Browne, and they had six children. From 1946 to 1947 he was an active member of the Crypt Group of Artists, St Ives, and in 1949 he was a founder member of Penwith Society of Arts in Cornwall.

In the summer of 1948 he travelled around Italy, held his first one-man exhibition at the Lefevre Gallery, London in 1950, and taught at the Bath Academy of Art, Corsham until 1957. He was invited by the Arts Council to contribute to their Festival of Britain exhibition in 1953, and was elected member of the Newlyn Society of Artists. In 1954 he was awarded the Critics Prize, by the British section of the International Association of Art Critics. From 1955 to 1960 he ran an art school, St Peter's Loft, at St Ives with Terry Frost and William Redgrave. In 1957 he visited New York for his first one-man show in America, at the Catherine Viviano Gallery, which brought him into contact with a new circle of artists, critics and collectors. He greatly admired the new American painting he saw in the Tate Gallery's exhibition of Modern Art in the United States, and on his trip to New York the work of Mark Rothko had particularly thrilled him. While he had long admired and been influenced by the English landscape tradition, American art encouraged him to adopt a looser and more open kind of painting. In 1959 he was awarded second prize at the John Moores Exhibition, Liverpool.

In 1961 he was elected Chairman of the Newlyn Society of Artists, and made a Bard of the Cornish Gorsedd for services to Cornish art. In 1962 he was commissioned to paint a mural for the house of Stanley J. Seeger in New Jersey. The following year he spent three months as visiting painter at the San Antonio Art Institute, Texas, and visited Mexico, followed by visits to Prague and Bratislava to lecture for the British Council.

By this time he had taken up gliding, in order 'to get a more complete knowledge of the landscape'. In the words of William Gaunt, reviewing an exhibition of Cornish painting in *The Times* in May 1968, the experience 'gave a heightened sense of space to the works of his last years'. Unfortunately it also resulted in his premature demise. While flying solo his plane nosedived into a runway at Dunkeswell airfield, Devon, on 27 August 1964. He was taken to hospital at Taunton, suffering from a fractured spine, and died from his injuries four days later.

Bernard Leach

Potter

Bernard Howell Leach was born in Hong Kong on 5 January 1887, son of Andrew Leach, a barrister and judge. His mother Eleanor died while giving birth to him. After his father married a distant cousin of Eleanor Leach in 1891 he took Bernard to Singapore. He returned to England to attend Beaumont Jesuit College, Windsor, and the Slade School of Fine Art, London. When his father was dying of cancer, Bernard promised to study for a career in banking, but he hated it and went to the London School of Art instead. He and his cousin Muriel moved to Japan in 1909 and married shortly afterwards. Befriending a group of young Japanese art lovers who called themselves Shirakaba, he began potting and learnt the rudiments of the art, painting on pots, and techniques of high-fired stoneware and porcelain. In 1914 he held a one-person show of pots, paintings, fabrics, and furniture in Tokyo and published his first book, *A Review, 1909–1914*, containing poems, prose, illustrations of his pots and reproductions of etchings. Three years later he set up a pottery in Japan; when it was burnt to the ground a helpful patron provided him with a new workshop and kiln, and two skilled potters to work under his direction.

After staging another exhibition he returned to England in 1920, so the children could be educated there. With him and the family came Shoji Hamada, a Tokyo potter who helped him set up the Leach Pottery near St Ives in partnership with a local philanthropist, Frances Horne. Local workmen helped them build a cottage and studio and construct a traditional Japanese wood-burning climbing kiln, the first of its type to be built in the west. They promoted pottery as a combination of Western and Eastern arts and philosophies, focusing on traditional Korean, Japanese and Chinese pottery, combined with traditional European techniques such as slipware and salt glaze-ware. At first they struggled financially, helped mainly by successful exports of pots and drawings to Japan. The pottery was narrowly rescued from closure by Leonard and Dorothy Elmhirst at Dartington, Devon, who invited Leach to move the business to their estate in south Devon. In 1932 he set up a small pottery there, but kept the main pottery open at St Ives. His eldest son David had joined the latter in 1930 and introduced innovations including converting the kiln from firing with wood to oil, and adding a range of tablewares that became known as standard ware.

In 1934 Leach returned briefly to Japan, touring potteries and collecting material for *A Potter's Book* (1940), including his thoughts on standards for studio pottery. After the war he visited Scandinavia, the United States, Canada, Australia and New Zealand, exhibiting his pots, giving talks, slide and film shows. He helped to organise an international pottery and weaving conference at Dartington in 1952, which included exhibitions of British pottery and textiles since 1920.

In 1956 he married Janet Darnell, who ran the pottery after David Leach's departure in 1955 to set up his own workshop. He became a freeman of St Ives in 1968, CBE in 1966 and CH in 1974. Around 1973 his eyesight failed and he stopped making and decorating pots, concentrating more on his writing. Among his later titles were *Kenzan and his Tradition* (1966), *The Unknown Craftsman: a Japanese Insight into Beauty* (1972), *Drawings, Verse and Belief* (1973), and *Beyond East and West: Memoirs, Portraits and Essays* (1978), a series of autobiographical writings about his life and art. The Victoria and Albert Museum in London held a major exhibition of his art in 1977. He died on 6 May 1979 at St Ives, and was buried there in Longstone Cemetery.

John le Carré (David Cornwell)

Author

David John Moore Cornwell was born on 19 October 1931 in Poole, Dorset, son of Ronnie and Olive Cornwell. His father was a confidence trickster who served a prison sentence for fraud, and younger sister Charlotte became a renowned actress. He studied foreign languages at the University of Berne and at Oxford where he graduated with a BA (Hons) in 1956. After teaching at Eton for two years, he spent five years working for the British Foreign Service, initially as second secretary in the British Embassy in Bonn, before being transferred to Hamburg for service as a political consul, and recruited into MI6. His career as a secret agent was destroyed during the Cold War by double agent Kim Philby, who gave Cornwell's name and others to the Russian KGB.

By then he had written his first novel, *A Call for the Dead,* published in 1961 under the pseudonym John le Carré, as were all his subsequent writings. While working in Europe he had met crime novelist John Bingham, who encouraged him to write, and read the manuscript of his first novel. Bingham, the pen-name and family name of Lord Clanmorris, was one of two men who provided the inspiration for le Carré's famous character, George Smiley, the other being a former rector at Lincoln College, Oxford. Some years later, in *Tinker, Tailor, Soldier, Spy*, le Carré based Gerald, the mole hunted by George Smiley, on Philby's weakness and deceit.

His second novel, *A Murder of Quality*, was a detective novel set in a boys' school, though the majority of his novels (apart from the partly autobiographical *The Naïve and Sentimental Lover*) were spy-thrillers, set during the Cold War. After the success of his third book, *The Spy Who Came in From the Cold* (1963), he devoted himself full-time to writing. He lived on the Greek islands for a few years and then returned to England, settling at St Buryan. In later works, including *The Honourable Schoolboy* and *The Night Manager*, he approached his material more as novelist and less as a mystery writer, focusing on the in-depth development of his characters. In *A Small Town in Germany*, set in Bonn where he had worked, most of the story was told in the form of dialogue between the major characters.

Critics and students of modern literature consider Le Carré's work a reasoned response to the lurid sensationalism of the James Bond genre of spy writing. His heroes are three-dimensional, their engagement with the world more realistic, amd their circumstances markedly unglamorous, with little of the 'action thriller' in his stories.

A Perfect Spy (1986), his most autobiographical novel, dealt with the author's peculiar relationship with his father. In 1965 *The Spy Who Came in From the Cold* became the first of his titles to be filmed. The following year *Call for the Dead* was adapted for the screen from *The Deadly Affair*. Several of his other titles have subsequently been adapted for film and television, his favourite being the BBC's dramatisation in 1979 of *Tinker, Tailor, Soldier, Spy*, starring Alec Guinness as George Smiley. A sequel came three years later when Guinness returned to the role in the BBC's *Smiley's People*.

In January 2003 he published an essay in *The Times* protesting against the war in Iraq, 'The United States has gone mad'. He has declined several honours, including a knighthood.

George Lloyd

Composer

George Walter Selwyn Lloyd was born in St Ives on 28 June 1913. His father William was a flautist and his mother played several string instruments. He started writing music when he was ten, and had decided to be a composer by the age of fourteen, but as he missed much of his schooling through rheumatic fever, he asked to leave school and concentrate on music. When the family moved to London he studied composition and violin. His *Symphony No. 1 in A minor*, written when he was nineteen, was premiered by the Bournemouth Symphony Orchestra in 1933. *Symphony No. 2 in E major* had its premier at Eastbourne in 1935 and was followed by *Symphony No. 3 in F major*, performed by the BBC Symphony Orchestra. His First opera *Iernin* had been performed in Penzance in 1934. An enthusiastic review in *The Times* by Frank Howes, led to London performances the following year. A second opera, *The Serf,* was staged at Covent Garden in 1938 under the baton of Albert Coates.

In the war as Royal Marine bandsman, Lloyd doubled as a gunner, serving on the notoriously dangerous Arctic convoys. In 1942 a faulty torpedo blew up his ship and after having seen most of his fellow gunners drowned in oil he was rescued. The trauma and severe shell shock exacerbated the weak health he had suffered as a child, bringing about a complete collapse. He tried to come to terms with his wartime experience in his *Symphony No. 4 in B major* and *Symphony No. 5*, works which only the devoted nursing of his wife Nancy enabled him to complete in 1946 and 1948 respectively. Despite illness he produced a third opera, *John Socman*, about a Wiltshire soldier at Agincourt, commissioned for the Festival of Britain in 1951, and premiered at Bristol. As with his first two operas, the libretto was provided by his father.

In 1952 he settled in Dorset, spending the next few years as a market gardener growing mushrooms and carnations. He still composed, often rising at 4.30 a.m. to write music for three hours before beginning work on the farm. Yet he was increasingly disillusioned with the problems of getting his work performed any more, remarking that he sent scores to the BBC and they were usually returned without comment.

Nevertheless he was championed by conductors Charles Groves and Edward Downes and pianist John Ogden, for whom he wrote the first of four piano concertos, *Scapegoat*, in 1963. In 1969 the BBC accepted his *Symphony No. 8* for performance, and broadcast it eight years later. His *Symphony No. 6* was given at the Proms in 1981, the year that three of his other symphonies were recorded. A deal with the Albany Symphony Orchestra, New York State, led to several performances and recordings of various compositions, including concertos for violin and cello, bringing him an American audience and, in his words, 'All of a sudden buckets of dollars!' Among the new works recorded were his *Symphony No. 11* and *Symphonies No. 12*, first performed in 1986 and 1990. Other major new compositions included a large scale choral piece based on the Latin poem *Pervigilium Veneris, The Vigil of Venus*, premiered at the Festival Hall in 1989, nine years after its completion, and *A Symphonic Mass*, which he conducted at its premiere at the 1993 Brighton Festival.

In later years he suffered increasingly from heart trouble. His last work, a *Requiem*, the score inscribed, 'Written in memory of Diana, Princess of Wales', was completed three weeks before his death in hospital at Marylebone on 3 July 1998.

William Lovett

Chartist

William Lovett was born in Penzance on 6 May 1800. His father was drowned at sea before he was born. His mother, a strict Methodist, sent him to the local school, and at thirteen he was apprenticed to a local ropemaker. Two years later he took up the trade of a carpenter, and at twenty-one left Cornwall for London to find work with a cabinet-making company.

While attending evening classes at the London's Mechanics' Institute, he met the radical publishers Henry Hetherington and John Cleave, who introduced him to the socialist principles of Robert Owen. Lovett became a supporter of the Civil and Religious Library Association, and joined Hetherington and Cleave in the London Co-operative Trading Association. For a while he worked as the Co-operative Trading Association's storekeeper and in 1828 became secretary of the British Association for the Promotion of Co-operative Knowledge.

In 1831 he was chosen for service in the London Militia, and when he refused to be conscripted his furniture was seized. His reaction was to found the Anti-Militia Association, adopting the slogan 'No Vote, No Musket', which led to the government relaxing the regulations which required able-bodied men to be called upon to serve in the force. Convinced that parliamentary reform was now the most important issue facing working people, he joined the National Union of the Working Classes, to campaign actively for universal male suffrage, and also Robert Owen's Grand National Consolidated Trades Union. In March 1832 he was arrested by the police during a peaceful demonstration, but was released without charge.

In June 1836 Lovett, Hetherington, Cleave and James Watson formed the London Working Men's Association (LMWA). The LWMA's membership was restricted to 100 working men, although it admitted thirty-five honorary members including the later Chartist leader Feargus O'Connor. Other honorary members included radical MPs, but the LWMA was strictly a working-class organisation, unlike similar political groupings which had a mainly middle-class executive.

At one meeting in 1838 the LMWA leaders drew up a charter of political demands. When supporters of parliamentary reform held a convention the following year, he was chosen as the leader of the group now known as the Chartists. In 1839 he was arrested after making a speech in Birmingham, the authorities claiming that his description of the Metropolitan police as a 'bloodthirsty and unconstitutional force' was seditious libel. He was found guilty and sentenced to twelve months' imprisonment in Warwick Gaol, where he collaborated with fellow prisoner John Collins, on the book *Chartism, a New Organisation of the People*. After nine months Lovett refused to accept three months remission for good behaviour, on the grounds that to do so would be an admission of guilt. On his release in July 1840 he returned to Cornwall to recover, and retired from active politics.

The next year he formed the National Association for Promoting the Political and Social Improvement of the People, an educational body, to provide circulating libraries and help the working classes to better themselves. It was to be funded through a one penny per week subscription paid by Chartists who had signed the national petition, but it never had the popular support for which he had hoped. He also wrote school

textbooks, and an autobiography, *The Life and Struggles of William Lovett* (1877), and taught evening classes. The bookshop he opened in Tottenham Court Road proved a failure and he died in poverty on 8 August 1877.

Richard Lower

Physician

Richard Lower was born in 1631 on the family estate at Tremeer House, near Bodmin. He was educated at Westminster School, and Christ Church, Oxford, where he graduated BA in 1653, MA in 1655, and BM and MD in 1665. While at Oxford, he was praelector in Greek (1656–7) and censor in natural philosophy (1657–60), and by 1659 he had established an active medical practice there. In 1667 he followed Thomas Willis, founder of the Royal Society, to London where he established a successful practice in London, first in Hatton Garden, next near Fleet Street, then Bow Street, and lastly King Street, near Covent Garden.

He and Willis worked jointly on investigating the human nervous system, while at the same time Lower began his own research on the heart. He traced the circulation of blood as it passed through the lungs, learned that it changed when exposed to air, and was the first to observe the difference in arterial and venous blood. He is generally credited with being the first to perform successful blood transfusions though his studies in this field were a logical continuation of work by Christopher Wren and Robert Boyle, who a few years earlier had successfully injected medication into the bloodstream of dogs. He was involved in some of the earliest experiments with blood transfusions, demonstrating that blood could be transfused from animal to animal and from animal to man intravenously. In 1665 he successfully performed the first direct blood transfusion, involving the transfer of blood from the carotid artery of one live dog into the jugular vein of another. He thus proved that the procedure was not only possible, but also effective in reviving an animal that would otherwise have died from severe blood loss.

After his experiments on dogs, he undertook transfusions of blood into a human subject, making him the first Western scientist to undertake such an operation. In 1667 he took part in an experiment to transfuse sheep's blood into a man who was mentally ill, as he believed the man could be helped either by the infusion of fresh blood or by the removal of old blood. The dog transfusion experiments were repeated before the Royal Society at Gresham College, London, and with the help of an associate, Dr Edmund King, he transfused sheep blood into a volunteer, Arthur Coga of Cambridge.

In 1669 he published *Tractatus de Corde*, which contained the results of his research into the anatomical and physiological structure and action of the heart, and a summary of his pioneering work in blood transfusion. His anatomical and physiological investigation of the structure and action of the heart was seen as an early breakthrough and he was considered one of the most skilled vivisectionists of his time. He was elected a Fellow of the Royal Society in 1667, and in 1671 he was a Member of the Royal College of Physicians, becoming a Fellow in 1675.

That same year he was appointed royal physician, and was in attendance on King Charles II during his last illness in 1685. Nevertheless, by then he had fallen out of favour at court because of his Whig sympathies and his anti-Catholic beliefs, which led to his loss of court appointments and a decline in his reputation and practice. Actively opposed to the policies of the pro-Catholic James II, he spent much of his time in Cornwall during the latter's brief reign, but after the revolution of 1688 he returned to court, giving advice on medical services for the navy. He died at his house in London on 17 January 1691 and was buried at St Tudy.

Sir William Lower

Politician and Natural Philosopher

Sir William Lower was born around 1570, eldest of six sons of Thomas and Jane Lower of St Winnow, near Lostwithiel. In 1586 he matriculated at Exeter College, Oxford. In 1589 he entered the Middle Temple, where he was frequently reprimanded for unruly behaviour. He was returned as MP for Bodmin in 1601, and for Lostwithiel in 1604, for seven years. That same year he and his brothers Nicholas and Francis were knighted by King James I. He married Penelope, stepdaughter of Henry Percy, 9th Earl of Northumberland, probably soon after he moved to London in 1601. As part of the marriage settlement he acquired about 3,000 acres in Carmarthenshire, including a home farm in Tra'venti, near Laugharne.

Lower and Northumberland were present at a dinner on 4 November 1605, the eve of the Gunpowder Plot in which a group of Catholics tried to kill King James and most of the Protestant aristocracy by blowing up the Houses of Parliament the next day. When government agents conducted their investigations after its failure, both men were interrogated about their conversation that night, though they had not been connected in the conspiracy and their innocence was clearly established.

As Northumberland was a patron of the scientist and mathematician Thomas Harriot, Lower formed a close friendship with Harriot and became his eager pupil, studying a variety of subjects including astronomy, mathematics, algebra, advanced geometry, trigonometry and alchemy. Between 17 September and 6 October 1607, from Lower, Carmarthenshire, regularly observed with the naked eye Halley's Comet on what with hindsight was one of its earliest recognised periodic appearances, and used a cross-staff to measure its position in relation to the stars. His first observation was made as he was on board ship sailing across the Bristol Channel to Wales, and he made an effort to follow it every night as often as weather permitted. He sent his measurements to Harriot at Syon House, who also made his own calculations on the matter.

Later he later took to observing the sky regularly through a telescope, working with his friend John Protheroe of Nantyrhebog, Carmarthenshire, and establishing an observatory on high ground near his house. In a letter to Harriot written in February 1610, he described in some detail the appearance of the Moon through his telescope, saying that, 'In the full she appears like a tart that my cooke made me last weeke; here a vaine of bright stuffe, and there of darke, and so confusedlie all over. I must confess I can see none of this without my cylinder.'

While on a visit to Syon House in December 1610, he and Harriot observed the satellites of Jupiter. His suggestion that year to Harriot that Kepler's elliptical orbits for the planets might also apply to comets is generally considered to be the earliest surviving record of what is now the accepted theory of comet orbits.

He died at Tra'venti on 12 April 1615, on the same day as his mother, Jane, leaving his wife, a daughter, Dorothy, and a posthumous son, Thomas.

Sir William Lower

Playwright and Translator

William Lower was born about 1609-10, the only son of John Lower of Tremere and his first wife, Jane. Little is known of his early life, though he is thought to have been baptised at Constantine and studied at Oxford for a while. In 1639 he published his first play, *The Phoenix in her Flames*, a tragic romance set in Arabia, dedicated to his cousin Thomas. His literary career was interrupted by military service in the royalist cause. He was appointed a lieutenant in the regiment of Sir Jacob Ashley in the Earl of Northumberland's army in 1640, and later that year, as a captain, he reported on his company's mutiny near Brackley.

During the civil war he was a lieutenant-colonel in the royal army and lieutenant-governor of Wallingford. In June 1644 the King ordered him to levy a weekly tax of £50 on the town of Reading for the Wallingford garrison. When the town refused to pay, Lower kidnapped the mayor of Reading as a hostage. The town's aldermen declared they were unable to pay and Lower tried unsuccessfully to reach a compromise, only resolved when the council of war at Oxford remitted part of the levy. In March 1645 he was knighted; in January 1646 he was captured by the parliamentary garrison of Abingdon and sent to London as a prisoner, remaining there for a year before being discharged and allowed to go overseas, on condition that he did nothing treasonable against the Parliamentary cause.

Around this time he married and had a daughter Elizabeth. He probably spent some time in the Low Countries, since his uncle Sir Nicholas Lower owned lands in Holland and Zeeland. Sir Nicholas died in 1653, leaving most of his estate to Sir William and his cousin Thomas, but they had difficulty in laying claim to their inheritance because of the wars. Lower was in England in July 1654 petitioning for permission to go to the Low Countries to settle his uncle's estate, but had to wait more than a year before it was granted. He was in The Hague by October 1655, and remained there for the next six years.

While in the Low Countries he began to translate and publish various French works. These included three non-dramatic works of René de Ceriziers on religious martyrs, *The Innocent Lady* (1654), *The Innocent Lord* (1655), and *The Triumphant Lady* (1656), as well as two plays by Corneille, *Polyeuctes* (1655) and *Horatius* (1656), two by Paul Scarron, *Don Japhet of Armenia*, and *The Three Dorothies*, now lost, and two by Quinault, *The Noble Ingratitude* (1659) and *The Amorous Fantasme* (1660). He had always maintained close connections with the exiled members of the royal family during the interregnum, and those who had married foreign princes, and the latter two works were dedicated, respectively, to the Princess Royal of Orange, for whom he published a funeral elegy in 1661, and to Elizabeth, Queen of Bohemia. In 1660 he translated a French description of King Charles II's sojourn in Holland prior to the restoration that year. He also wrote another original play, *The Enchanted Lovers* (1658), and a manuscript set of paraphrases on the apostolic epistles.

Returning to England in 1661, he died early the following year. He was thought to have been buried either in St Clement Danes, Westminster, or in St Winnow, though no records of a burial place at either exist.

Thomas Luny

Painter

Thomas Luny, son of Thomas and Elizabeth Luny, was born in Cornwall, probably at St Ewe near Mevagissey, where he was baptised on 20 May 1759. He showed some artistic ability at an early age, and moved to London at about fourteen where he was apprenticed to the marine painter Francis Holman. Specialising in landscapes and seascapes, he first exhibited at the Society of Artists in 1777 and at the Royal Academy in 1780. In 1783 he exhibited *Battle of the Dogger Bank* there, and continued to show pictures annually until 1793, then again in 1802, when his *Battle of the Nile* was widely praised.

After moving to his own studio at Leadenhall Street in 1783 he made friends with Mr Merle, a dealer and framer who would have considerable success in promoting Luny's work. The British East India Co. had their headquarters nearby, and once his reputation was established, their officers commissioned several paintings and portraits from him. He was an occasional guest on the company's ships on special occasions and voyages, and took advantage of the opportunities to make sketches of overseas locations such as Naples, Gibraltar, and Charleston, South Carolina, all of which proved invaluable for his paintings once he arrived home.

In 1807 he moved to Teignmouth where the commissions continued, often for portraits of specific ships and scenes of particular naval engagements, mostly from former mariners and local gentry. Among them were two large pictures, *The Bombardment of Algiers* in 1816, painted in 1819 for Admiral Lord Exmouth, who kept them at his home, Canonteign House. Luny was so successful that two years later he was able to build a house in Teign Street, later known as Luny House. From February 1807 to December 1835 he kept a complete list of his paintings, purchasers, and prices, comprising over 2,200 works. It has been estimated that in his lifetime he produced over 3,000 pictures. The earliest listed included views of London and Blackfriars bridges, although scenes from Teignmouth and the Devonshire coastline predominated from June 1807. Picturesque local coastal views, shipping scenes, and naval events remained his favourite theme, with most selling for £5 or less, though larger ones commanded more, generally no more than £25.

By around 1820 he was beginning to suffer from arthritis in both hands, which eventually confined him to a wheelchair and forced him to work with his brush held between both fists or strapped to his wrist. He gave up painting completely around 1835, though his last pictures were shown at the Royal Academy in 1837, just before 130 were exhibited for sale in Old Bond Street. The last known date on one of his paintings is 1836. He also painted in watercolour and a number of his pictures, both naval and topographical, were engraved. The best public collections of his work are to be found in the National Maritime Museum, Greenwich, and the Royal Albert Memorial Museum, Exeter.

He died on 30 September 1837 at his home in Teignmouth, and was buried in West Teignmouth Churchyard.

Benjamin Luxon

Baritone

Benjamin Luxon was born in Redruth on 24 March 1937. After leaving school he went to study at the Guildhall School of Music and Drama, and soon established an international reputation as a singer when he won a third prize at the 1961 ARD International Music Competition in Munich. Shortly afterwards he joined the English Opera Group set up by composer Benjamin Britten, and on their tour of the Soviet Union in 1963 he sang the roles of Sid and Tarquinius in, respectively, Britten's operas *Albert Herring* and *The Rape of Lucretia*. He was chosen by Britten to sing the title role in his television opera *Owen Wingrave*, which also featured the English Opera Group, broadcast in May 1971.

In 1972 he made his first appearances at both the Royal Opera House, Covent Garden, creating the role of the Jester in Peter Maxwell Davies' opera *Taverner*, and at the Glyndebourne Opera Festival, where he sang the title role in Raymond Leppard's realization of Monteverdi's *Il Ritorno d'Ulisse*. As a result he became a regular guest at both venues and at Tanglewood in Massachusetts.

In 1974 he began a long and successful association with the English National Opera, culminating in his appearance in the title role of Verdi's *Falstaff* in 1992. He made his Metropolitan Opera début in Tchaikovsky's *Eugene Onegin* in 1980, his La Scala début in 1986 and his Los Angeles début in Berg's *Wozzeck* in 1988. During this time he sang in most of the major European opera houses, with frequent appearances at Bayerische Staatsoper, Munich, and Vienna Wiener Staatsoper, Vienna. In 1986 he was awarded a CBE for services to British music.

In addition to his opera work, he also developed a reputation as a concert-giver and recitalist with a broad repertoire which embraced early music, Lieder, contemporary song, music hall and folk music. He was also recognised for his work rehabilitating parlour songs from the late nineteenth and early twentieth century, particularly in partnership with noted tenor and conductor Robert Tear. He made over 100 recordings, many featuring early and mid twentieth-century British songwriting and folksong arrangements by composers such as Britten, George Butterworth,

Percy Grainger, Ivor Gurney, Roger Quilter, Ralph Vaughan Williams and Peter Warlock. Always keen not to be pigeonholed, he had said in 1974 that when he entered the business, he 'saw the danger of being put into one category or another; "Oh, he's an oratorio man, and he's a Verdi singer," and I didn't want any part of it.'

In 1990 he was struck by an affliction which left him with total loss of hearing in the left ear and distorted hearing in the right. Some years previously he had been diagnosed with Ménière's syndrome, and treatment left him with severe tinnitus.

It was now discovered that he had a rare disease of the immune system which could be suppressed but not cured by chemotherapy. After taking a short break for treatment he returned to a schedule of international engagements in 1992, with a sophisticated hearing aid in his right ear. Nevertheless, persistent fluctuation and deterioration in his hearing soon brought his career as a performer to a premature end. Loath to give up music altogether, he developed a new career as a narrator and poetry reader, while continuing to give masterclasses and direct opera.

Dame Moura Lympany

Concert Pianist

Mary Gertrude Johnstone was born on 18 August 1916 at Saltash, daughter of an army officer. She had her first piano lessons from her mother, a governess in pre-war St Petersburg, and at the age of six was went to a convent school in Belgium, where her musical talent was encouraged. Later she studied at Liège, and won a scholarship to the Royal Academy of Music in London, dividing her time between lessons there and a general education at a convent school in Kensington. In the summer of 1929 her mother took her to a concert at which a boy prodigy was playing a concerto with Basil Cameron conducting. She asked if she could play with the orchestra, and her mother wrote to Cameron requesting an audition for her. Just before her thirteenth birthday, she was invited to play Mendelssohn's *Piano Concerto No. 1 in G minor* in Harrogate with Cameron conducting. When he advised her to choose a more striking name, she changed Mary to Moura and add her mother's maiden name of Limpenny, adapting it to Lympany as it rhymed with timpani. She continued her piano studies in Vienna with Paul Weingarten while working as an au pair and in London with Mathilde Verne, a former pupil of Clara Schumann.

In 1944 she married Colin Defries, managing director of an engineering firm, an amateur pianist and a keen gardener, but they divorced in 1950. In 1951 she married Bennet H. Korn, an American television executive, and moved to America where she had two miscarriages (one of twins), and a premature son who only lived for two days. The couple divorced in 1961. Later she became a close friend of the future Prime Minister Edward Heath, a keen amateur musician, and there was occasional speculation that they might marry.

She made her American debut in 1948 and gave concerts and recitals throughout Europe and in Canada, South America, Australia, New Zealand and India. Throughout her professional life she practised for four hours a day, but no more, insisting that 'if you can't get it right in four you never will.' She said she played best after a good night's sleep and a good steak. In later years she divided her time between London, Monaco and her Pyrenean home Rasiguères in Languedoc where she had lived since 1973, and where she established an annual festival of music and wine between 1981 and 1992. In 1979 she celebrated the 50th anniversary of her concert debut with a Festival Hall recital attended by the Prince of Wales. She was appointed CBE in 1979 and DBE in 1992. *Moura: Her Autobiography*, written with her cousin, Margot Strickland, appeared in 1991. When invited as a castaway on BBC Radio 4's *Desert Island Discs*, she chose eight of her own recordings. She died at Menton, France, on 28 March 2005.

Andy Mackay

Musician

Andrew Mackay was born in Lostwithiel on 23 July 1946, but grew up in London. He discovered classical music at an early age thanks to his father, a talented amateur pianist, and rock'n'roll via the BBC Light Programme and Radio Luxembourg. After taking up oboe at Westminster City Grammar School, he won a scholarship to the Guildhall School of Music and played in the London Schools Symphony Orchestra. While reading music and English literature at Reading University he swopped his telescope, treasured since childhood, for an alto saxophone which he learnt while playing with university group the Nova Express. An interest in avant-garde and electronic music led to a meeting with Brian Eno, an art student at Winchester College, who became a close friend and colleague.

Mackay left university with a BA (Hons), and lived in Rome for a year, then returned to England and taught music at Holland Park Comprehensive School. While there he met singer Bryan Ferry, who was looking for musicians to form a group. They recruited Eno and various others, and by mid-1971 were playing gigs as Roxy. In 1972 they renamed themselves Roxy Music, recorded Radio 1 sessions for John Peel, and signed to EG Records. Their first album, *Roxy Music,* and debut single *Virginia Plain,* both made the Top 10 of their respective charts and established them as a major force on the music scene. Mackay's saxophone and oboe work were as much an integral part of the group as his striking visual image with sideburns and bleached blue-tipped quiff, and his onstage duckwalk during solos. Their first two albums were written solely by Ferry but from the third, *Stranded,* onwards, Mackay shared some writing credits, notably on *Love is the Drug,* a No. 2 single in 1975.

By then most members of the group had begun work on solo projects. Mackay's first album, *In Search of Eddie Riff* (1974), was in his words a showcase for his different musical interests, including classical, Motown, fifties rock, and country and western. He also played on two hit singles by Mott the Hoople, *Honaloochie Boogie* and *All the way from Memphis.* When Roxy Music went on hold in 1976 Mackay collaborated with playwright Howard Schuman on the television series *Rock Follies*, for which he wrote the music, and one of the two resulting soundtrack albums topped the charts in 1977. He also played on solo albums with Eno and Roxy guitarist Phil Manzanera, and released a second of his own. *Resolving Contradictions* (1978), inspired by a trip he and his wife Jane made to China, with guest appearances from Manzanera and Roxy Music drummer Paul Thompson. The group reformed in 1979 for a further three successful albums and a No.1 single, the John Lennon tribute *Jealous Guy,* before disbanding in 1983. Mackay and Manzanera then formed the Explorers, who released a couple of albums with limited success. In 1981 he published *Electronic Music: The Instruments, The Music & The Musicians*.

Between 1988 and 1991 he undertook a Bachelor of Divinity course at King's College, London and recorded a Christmas album in 1989, *Christmas*, with The Players, an English folk ensemble. Subsequent projects have included further television work, including music for *Armchair Thriller*, *Class Act* and *Hazell*, the soundtrack to the film *Velvet Goldmine*, various instrumental and relaxation albums, and sessions for other artists including Paul McCartney, the Pet Shop Boys, Mike Oldfield, John Cale, Yukihiro Takahashi, and inevitably Bryan Ferry. He took part in concerts with further reformations of Roxy Music in 2001, 2003 and Live 8 in 2005, as well as working on an as yet unreleased Roxy album.

Nigel Martyn

Footballer

Antony Nigel Martyn was born on 11 August 1966 in St Austell. He began his career as a midfielder until the age of sixteen when he was invited to play as a goalkeeper for his brother's works team. Later while playing at amateur level for St Blazey he was 'spotted' by the Bristol Rovers' tea lady while she was on holiday, and this led to the start of his professional career with the team in 1987. Two years later he became the first goalkeeper to attract a £1 million transfer fee in English football when he joined Crystal Palace. He remained there for seven seasons, playing 349 matches including the 1990 FA Cup final, where Crystal Palace were beaten by Manchester United after a 3-3 draw on a hard-fought replay, and the 1991 Zenith Data Systems Cup final, where Crystal Palace beat Everton.

When he made his debut for the England national side in Moscow in 1992, he became one of the few Cornishmen to play for England. He earned only twenty-three caps for his national side, spending the peak of his career as second-choice goalkeeper behind David Seaman.

In 1996 he signed with Leeds United, establishing another record fee for a goalkeeper of £2.25 million, and was the team's first-choice goalkeeper for six seasons. In the summer of 2003 Leeds were approached by Chelsea and Everton with offers to sign Martyn. Both clubs were offering him a backup post: at Chelsea, where he would understudy Carlo Cudicini; at Everton, the first-choice was Richard Wright. Martyn joined Everton in September 2003, and six games into the season, Wright sustained an injury which enabled Martyn to make his Everton debut. His performances for the first team during Wright's recovery were so good that Martyn remained Everton's first-choice goalkeeper even after Wright returned from injury.

He was one of Everton's strongest performers in the 2004-05 season when they achieved their best-ever finish in the Premier League, of fourth. Many fans were sure that he almost single-handedly stopped them from slipping down the league table after Thomas Gravesen's departure, and he produced some of the best form of his career. In 2005 he was voted as one of the players chosen by Crystal Palace fans as part of their Centenary XI, players whom they considered their favourites during the history of the club, in a poll celebrating the club's centenary. In April 2006 he featured in a similar poll for Leeds United, being chosen as part of their greatest team. Over 6ft tall, he was affectionately known by fans as 'Big Nige'.

During his career he played over 800 senior games during spells with Bristol Rovers, Crystal Palace, Leeds United and Everton, as well as winning twenty-three caps for England. In January 2006 he was put out of action by a stress fracture, and hoped to resume playing, but in June he announced that he intended to retire from professional football due to a persistent ankle injury. Plans to take up goalkeeper coaching instead were frustrated for a similar reason.

Edward Meredith

Jesuit

Edward Meredith was born in 1648, probably in Landulph, son of Edward, the local Anglican rector, and his wife Alice Kekewitch. In 1661 he was sent to Westminster School and four years later went to Christ Church, Oxford, but left in 1668, apparently without taking a degree. In the following year he went to Spain as secretary to Sir William Godolphin, a distant relation, who had been sent there as ambassador, and while there both men joined the Roman Catholic faith in 1671. He returned to England that summer and participated in religious debates with the Anglican clergyman Edward Stillingfleet, a future dean of St Paul's, the discussions being published in 1687 as *The Sum of the Conference between Two Divines*. Until 1684 he received an annual pension of £100 from Godolphin who, he said, had 'told me he looked upon me as his son'.

He is thought to have left England again at the time of the Popish Plot. In 1682 he published a pamphlet, *Some Remarques upon a Late Popular Piece of Nonsence called Julian the Apostate*, in defence of the staunchly Catholic and increasingly unpopular Duke of York and the principles of passive resistance against attacks from the ardent Whig apologist, Samuel Johnson, who had published a fierce indictment of the heir to the throne. Two years later he joined the Society of Jesus, as his brother Amos had done, taking the name Edward Langsford, and enrolled at the noviciate at Watten, Flanders. He remained a Jesuit for the rest of his life, though he was never ordained.

The accession of King James II made him feel more comfortable in England and he returned to London in 1686, publishing a number of pro-Catholic pamphlets during the next two years. He was also involved in controversial exchanges with Protestant pamphleteers, and in several oral debates which took place between Catholic and Protestant theologians. He also published a translation from a selection of Catholic meditative passages, *A Journal of Meditations for every day of the year*. In 1687 he was among a number of fellows sympathetic to the King's views on Magdalen College, Oxford, which the latter tried to impose on the college.

During the revolution of 1688 he fled from England and joined the Jacobite settlement at St Germain-en-Laye. He moved to the Jesuit establishment in Rome in 1696, and to Naples around 1702, though he also spent some time in Paris and at the English College, Rome. By this time his eyesight and general health were failing. During his last years he worked to secure a benefaction for the English school at St Omer from the estate of Godolphin, who had made him a trustee for a fund of 4,000 Spanish doubloons in his will.

In a letter dated early 1715 he defended and emphasised his adherence to the Jacobite cause, claiming that the example of King George I, who had been called to the British throne a year earlier, was 'now the strongest motive for conversion'. He died at Rome probably later the same year, leaving detailed instructions in his will for the use of Godolphin's trust funds in repaying his debts and in helping English Catholics.

John Miller

Painter

John Miller was born in London on 30 July 1931 and spent most of his adult life in Penzance. He worked at several jobs before deciding to become a full-time painter. After his National Service, he was briefly an actor in films, theatre and television. In the early 1950s he ran a coffee bar and restaurant, L'Elixir, on Richmond Hill, Surrey, with his close friend and constant companion, Michael Truscott, the potter, picture-framer and restorer, as its chef, until it was demolished as part of a road-widening scheme. Soon after that, having started studying as an architect, with particular reference to church architecture, he went to Cornwall to work on St Buryan Church. He became thoroughly enamoured with the area and in 1958, though they only had a few pounds between them, he and Truscott crossed the River Tamar in an old Austin Seven and drove to the far west of Cornwall, where they decided to make their home.

Turning from architecture to painting, he became a member of the Newlyn Society of Artists in 1961, and three years later he was elected a Fellow of the Royal Society of Arts. His regular visits to the Isles of Scilly inspired a series of beach paintings, and after living at Sancreed for many years he painted from a house on the beach at Lelant, where some of his most evocative paintings were executed. Travels further afield to such destinations as Venice, Goa and Greece also influenced much of his work. As a contemporary landscape artist he was known particularly for the blues and yellows of sky, sand and sea, and his pictures were often used on posters, cards and CD covers, including that of Chris Rea's *King of the Beach*.

In 2001 his seventieth birthday exhibition at the Portland Gallery, London, was a sell-out. By this time his blue paintings of sky, sea and sand, of the Hayle Estuary and of Tresco, Isles of Scilly, had become very popular and were virtually his trademark. Always ready to encourage young artists, each year he conducted a 'Looking, Seeing and Drawing' course at the Cerne Abbas Friary of St Francis. He was also a lay canon of Truro Cathedral.

In 1989, he published an autobiography, *Leave Tomorrow Behind*. He died of cancer on 23 July 2002. A memorial exhibition included a selection of paintings inspired by the last trip he made to Goa, as well as his characteristic works of Cornwall in oil and gouache.

David Mudd

Politician and Journalist

William David Mudd was born in Falmouth on 2 June 1933, and educated at Truro Cathedral School. His father William was a naval captain, and he joined the Merchant Navy before going into journalism. He was a staff reporter with the *Tavistock Gazette*, a member of the *Western Morning News* editorial staff, and editor of *The Cornish Echo* for two years. As a staff announcer and commentator he also became familiar to viewers on local BBC television and Westward (ITV).

Between 1963 and 1965 he was a member of Tavistock Urban District Council. Entering politics, he stood as a Conservative for Falmouth and Camborne in the 1970 election and won the constituency from Labour with a majority of 1,523. A large personal vote helped him to transform a moderately safe Labour seat since the Second World War into a comfortable Conservative one, and in 1979 he increased his majority to 16,600. In 1973 he became Secretary of the Conservative West Country Committee, a post he held for three years, and served in a similar capacity on his party's Fisheries Sub-Committee from 1974 to 1975.

When his party returned to government in 1979 he was appointed Parliamentary Private Secretary at the Department of Energy during the period of offshore oil development, but returned to the backbenches in protest in 1981 after the annual budget

imposed heavy increases on fuel duty, saying that it would penalise rural areas such as Cornwall. Throughout his years in the Commons he became known as something of a maverick, ever since he had voted in 1971 against Britain joining the Common Market. Later, he admitted that he resented 'conforming to the party line, party policy, and government edicts'. In 1986, when the government came under fire for their handling of the crisis in the Cornish tin industry after Geevor mine closed, and three others were threatened due to lack of financial help, he voted with the opposition, as he did two years later when plans to impose dental charges were debated.

At the same time he established a reputation as a writer, mainly of local history, beginning in 1971 with his first book, *Cornishmen and True*, on famous men of the county. It was followed by several other titles about the locality, including *Cornish Sea Lights* (1978), *About the City: Portrait of Truro* (1979), *Around and About the Roseland* (1980), *The Cruel Cornish Sea* (1981), *The Cornish Edwardians* (1982), and *Around and About the Fal* (1989). He also wrote about his neighbouring county in *Dartmoor Reflections* (1993) and *The Magic of Dartmoor* (1994). *Better With a Pinch of Salt* (2003) was a volume of short stories.

'Falmouth is my town,' he wrote in *Home Along Falmouth and Penryn* (1980). 'I love it as a place in which history never ends and in which the ghosts of the past are but a flicker of time away.' In a 1993 interview he said he liked to believe that his books offered hope, 'reminding people through history that even the bleakest episodes of the past ultimately led to economic and social recovery.'

In 1989 he announced his decision to stand down from Parliament, so he could spend more time with his wife and devote himself increasingly to writing. Three weeks before the 1992 election, he revealed that he had resigned the party whip in the Commons a year earlier, in protest at the scale of the Cornish tin mining crisis and the government's withdrawal of £1.7 million aid to the struggling Wheal Jane mine. Since then he had sat as an Independent Conservative, saying that the government was probably good for Britain, 'but it isn't good for Cornwall'. In the 2005 election, thirteen years after leaving Westminster, he contested his old seat again as an Independent, standing on a 'People before politics' ticket and saying the electorate were 'fed up with party politics', but polled only 961 votes.

William Murdoch

Engineer

William Murdoch was born on 21 August 1754 at Cumnock, East Ayrshire, son of John Murdoch, a millwright, and educated in Scotland. As a boy he learned the principles of mechanics, and the basics of metalwork and woodwork from helping his father. In 1777 he joined the Watt & Boulton factory at Birmingham. Two years later he was sent to Redruth with responsibility for the building and maintenance of their engines, used for pumping water out of the Cornish tin mines. Several engine erectors in Cornwall were in fierce competition, with much copying of mechanical innovations and violation of patents. Murdoch assisted with legal action against some of the competitors, and inspected engines constructed by others, either to determine whether patents had been infringed or to assess their effectiveness.

He also dealt with mechanical problems related to steam engines, and made practical improvements to the basic designs. One of his most significant inventions was the sun and planet gear which allowed steam power to be used to 'produce a continued Rotative or Circular Motion round an Axis or Centre, and thereby to give Motion to the Wheels of Mills or other Machines'. It converted the vertical motion of a beam, driven by a small steam engine, into circular motion using a 'planet', a cogwheel fixed at the end of the pumping rod of the engine.

In 1784 he produced Britain's first working model of a steam-engine carriage, or locomotive, a three-wheeled vehicle 1ft high with the engine and boiler placed between the two larger back wheels, a spirit lamp underneath to heat the water and a tiller at the front turning the smaller front wheel. When he demonstrated it at the King's Head, Truro, it was the first public showing in Britain of steam locomotion in action. It is said that one night he had tested it outside on the open road and it outpaced him, leaving him to chase after it. As he did so he met an alarmed local clergyman who had mistaken his carriage, with billowing smoke and fire burning under the boiler, for the devil. He also carried out experiments in the field of chemistry and made several discoveries, including that of iron cement made from sal ammoniac, or ammonium chloride and iron filings, when he noticed that both components had accidentally mixed in his tool bag and formed a solid mass.

His most noteworthy invention was the application of gas lighting as a replacement for oil and tallow produced light. He had first experimented with the use of gas, derived from the heating of coal and other materials, for lighting in 1792. To use it for practical purposes he needed to develop a working method for its production and capture, and by 1794 he was producing coal gas from a small retort containing heated coals with an iron tube attached, through which he piped gas before sending it through an old gun barrel and igniting it to produce light. His house at Redruth was the first domestic residence lit by gas. Apart from the benefits of gas lighting and heating, the process for producing coal gas yielded other substances which were subsequently successfully exploited, including coke; ammonia; and phenol (carbolic acid), a disinfectant and one of the components of Bakelite. In 1799 he invented a simplified and more efficient steam wheel, a forerunner of the steam turbine.

In 1815 he designed and installed the first gravity-fed piped hot-water system since classical times at Leamington Spa Baths. Two years later he began designing and building steam-power engines for boats. He died on 15 November 1839 and was buried at St Mary's Church, Handsworth.

John Nettles

Actor

John Nettles was born in St Austell on 11 October 1943, and adopted at birth by Eric Nettles, a carpenter and his wife Elsie. At the age of seven he discovered that his mother was an Irish Catholic nurse who had been working in England during the First World War, was committed to a mental institution after he was born, and died of tuberculosis at twenty-eight. Though he never discovered the identity of his biological father, he found that he had a brother and two sisters. He was educated at St Austell Grammar School, and then studied history and philosophy at Southampton University, where he developed a taste for acting.

At the age of sixteen he took a holiday in the clay mines at St Austell, and in between acting roles he would periodically go back and work there. He also taught on occasion in an inner-city London school during the late 1960s and early 1970s, later saying that he considered it the worst job he ever had ever undertaken.

However, by this time his career as an actor was proving more fruitful. During the 1969–70 season he was in repertory at the Northcott Theatre, Exeter, and in 1970 made his film acting debut in the comedy *One More Time*, followed later by another appearance in the western *The Red, White and Black*. A year later he took the role of Dr Ian Mackenzie in the period drama *A Family at War*. Following that he had roles in several TV series including *The Adventures of Black Beauty, The Liver Birds, Enemy at the Door* and *Robin of Sherwood*. He married his first wife, Joyce, in 1966. They had a daughter Emma, and divorced in 1979.

From 1981 to 1991 he played the part of Jim Bergerac in the crime drama *Bergerac*, set on Jersey, one of the most successful series of its kind, which ran for eighty-seven episodes. Next he did five seasons with the Royal Shakespeare Co., appearing in *The Winter's Tale, The Merry Wives of Windsor, Julius Caesar, Richard III* and *The Devil is an Ass*, as well as television adaptations of Shakespeare. His subsequent television roles included parts in an episode of *Boon, Heartbeat, The Hound of the Baskervilles* and as Jim Bergerac in the spoof police comedy *The Detectives*. In July 1995 he married Cathryn Sealey, whom he had met while in pantomime.

Also in 1995 he was approached to play Tom Barnaby in the murder mystery series, *Midsomer Murders*. It became the most successful role of his career, with over sixty episodes made from 1997 to date. In 2003 he played Barnaby in the Boxing Day episode of *French & Saunders*. He has been much in demand as a narrator for television documentary series including *Airport, Tourist Trap, Fraud Squad and The Millennium Time-Bomb,* and various audio books. In addition to his success as an actor he has also enjoyed a career as an author, having written three books, *Bergerac's Jersey, John Nettles' Jersey* and *Nudity in a Public Place*. In 2007 he appeared in the BBC Radio 4 comedy series *Will Smith Presents the Tao of Bergerac* alongside comedian Will Smith.

Percy Lane Oliver

Founder of the First Voluntary Blood Donor Service

Percy Lane Oliver was born on 11 April 1878 at his maternal grandparents' home in Fish Street, St Ives, the son of Edward Lane Oliver and his wife Jane, who were teachers in Maidenhead. In 1883 the family moved to London, and he was educated at a Wesleyan school at Camberwell. In 1893 he passed first out of 450 entrants for the civil service entrance examination but was rejected on medical grounds. He became an assistant librarian with Camberwell Borough Council, and joined the Town Hall staff in 1901. He became a founding member of the Camberwell division of the British Red Cross Society, and honorary secretary in 1910. During the First World War he and his wife Ethel, whom he had married in 1905, worked on behalf of Belgian refugees. In 1916 the family moved into rooms over the division's headquarters in Talfourd Road, London, and he joined the Royal Naval Air Service, stationed at Crystal Palace. For their war work he and his wife received the OBE in 1918.

Blood transfusions, formerly used in military situations, were used increasingly in civilian medicine after the First World War. Surgeons who wished to transfuse blood needed a donor at once. Oliver had the idea of forming a panel of donors in 1921, after four members of his Red Cross division responded to a call from King's College Hospital but found only one was of a suitable blood group. He asked for volunteers to have their blood group tested and be prepared to attend a hospital whenever a call came through, day or night. In 1922 the panel responded to thirteen calls from hospitals, by 1927 almost 1,300 calls, and by 1938 around 6,000 calls. By this time there were about 2,700 donors on the panel. They were unpaid, with initial costs being covered mainly by donations. Dr Geoffrey Keynes, medical adviser to Oliver's service, insisted that donors should not be regarded as heroes, though in order to provide some incentive Oliver devised a system of rewarding donors with certificates and medals.

From 1926 a joint committee of doctors, donors, and Red Cross headquarters personnel supervised the Greater London Red Cross Blood Transfusion Service. Oliver and his wife continued to run the service from their home at Peckham Rye, with some help; he often worked seven days a week, dealing with paperwork and telephoning volunteers. In 1928 the family moved to larger premises at Colyton Road, London. In 1933 he took early retirement from Camberwell Borough Council to run the service full-time and travel around the country lecturing. Panels were established in many cities, and he helped organise multiple donor sessions at hospitals. By the outbreak of the Second World War, the move from panels providing donors on call to blood banks had begun, and the wartime Emergency Blood Transfusion Service organised mass appeals and built up large blood banks.

Despite support from many eminent surgeons and doctors, some resented a layman's intrusion into medical matters. Oliver had to try hard to dispel apprehensions, and in February 1940 he gave an illustrated lecture in St Ives where the area secretary of Toc-H asked those present 'not to stand in the way of would-be donors, but rather to go out and radiate the wonderful work that had been done and was being done by blood transfusion'.

He died at St George's Hospital, Westminster, on 16 April 1944. In 1992 a plaque was placed on his birthplace in St Ives.

William Oliver

Physician and Inventor of the Bath Oliver Biscuit

William Oliver was born at Ludgvan, near Penzance, on 4 August 1695, the second son of John and Mary Oliver of Trevarno, Sithney, Cornwall. He was educated at Pembroke College, Cambridge, graduating MB in medicine in 1720, then went to the University of Leiden in 1720. After a few years in Europe he returned to England and took his MD at Cambridge in 1725. He first practised as a physician in Plymouth, where in 1724 he introduced smallpox inoculation, still a relatively new technique.

About 1725 he moved to Bath with his Cornish cousin, the Revd Walter Borlase. On arrival he lived in Westgate Street, but as he became more successful he acquired a grand house on the west side of Queen Square. Soon after settling in Bath he befriended Ralph Allen, a fellow Cornishman, and his social circle soon included the poet Alexander Pope and other famous people of the day. He was elected a Fellow of the Royal Society in 1730. He contributed brief papers to the Philosophical Transactions, and in 1751 published *A Practical Essay on the Use and Abuse of Warm Water Bathing in Gouty Cases*.

In 1753 he published a 'pastoral', *Myra*, and wrote a number of poems. He was also the anonymous author of *A Faint Sketch of the Life, Manner and Character of the Late Mr. Nash* which was praised by Oliver Goldsmith as 'written with much good sense and still more good nature.' He had interests besides medicine. Contemporaries recognized him as a 'civilized personality', fascinated by books, painting, and architecture.

He took great pains to obtain subscriptions for the building of the Water or General Hospital, later the Royal Mineral Water Hospital, at Bath, and in 1737 made an offer of some land for its site. The following year he was appointed one of the treasurers to the hospital fund, and in July 1739 he became a deputy president. He was one of the main founders of the Bath General Hospital, now the Royal National Hospital for Rheumatic Diseases, with Ralph Allen, John Wood and Richard (Beau) Nash. Elected physician to the hospital in May 1740, he drew up regulations for the admission and discharge of English patients, and in 1756 he compiled a comparable set of rules for patients from Scotland and Ireland. He played a major role in the government of the institution until he resigned in 1761, by which time he had attended over 600 meetings of the weekly management committee. In 1760 he put together a collection of *Cases of the Persons Admitted into the Infirmary at Bath under the Care of Doctor Oliver*.

He is probably best remembered for having invented the English Bath Oliver biscuit. At first he produced the Bath Bun, a rich confectionery that his patients whom he was treating for rheumatism greatly enjoyed, but then found that the product was making them too fat, so after experimenting he came up with the plainer, less fattening Bath Oliver biscuit instead.

For some years he suffered from gout. He died at Bath on 17 March 1764, and was buried in the churchyard of All Saints, Weston. It is said that he willed the recipe for Bath Olivers to his coachman Atkins, together with a sack of flour and a sum of money.

John Opie

Painter

John Opie was born in May 1761 at Blowing House, Mithian, St Agnes, near Truro, the son of Edward Opie, a mine carpenter, and his wife Mary. His interest in drawing developed early but he was also academically inclined. He was educated at the village school where he was an excellent scholar, and was teaching mathematics to the other children by the time he was twelve, when he opened an evening school for arithmetic and writing. He had already shown skill in drawing and painting, by copying a landscape belonging to a friend, and by producing a portrait of his own father. The latter did not want him to follow such a trade, and early on bound him as his own apprentice and subsequently to a sawyer.

At about fifteen he was befriended by Dr John Wolcot of Truro, an amateur artist and critic, who took him into his own house in Truro and gave him some coaching. In 1780 he was taken to London and introduced as 'The Cornish Wonder,' a self-taught genius. Wolcot ensured that he should not become too refined, believing that his attraction and eventual success as an artist in London lay in presenting him as 'a wild animal of St Agnes, caught among the tin-works.' He introduced him to Sir Joshua Reynolds and his former pupil James Northcote, who became a lifelong friend and once said, 'Other artists paint to live; Opie lives to paint.' He was presented to George III and Queen Charlotte, and the King bought two pictures. His first early success as a curiosity to the fashionable *beau monde* was thus succeeded by solid patronage, and he painted several portraits of the Hoare and Burrell families. His gift for child portraiture was seen in paintings of the Duke and Duchess of Argyll's children. One of his finest fancy pictures, *A Peasant's Family*, was painted around 1783, while he also received acclaim for *A School*.

He supplemented his early education by studying Latin, French and English literature, and polishing his provincial manners by mixing in cultivated and learned circles. In 1786 he exhibited his first important historical subject, *The Assassination of James I*, and in the next year *The Murder of Rizzio*. He was elected a full member of the Royal Academy in 1788. Meanwhile he was commissioned to paint subjects for the Shakespeare Gallery of John Boydell, who bought both historical pictures and presented them to the Guildhall, where they were destroyed in the Second World War.

His first marriage was dissolved in 1796, and two years later he married Amelia Alderson. After this he concentrated more on fancy pictures; he was frustrated by having to paint portraits for a living instead of history scenes, and having to teach.

His last historical painting was exhibited at the Royal Academy in 1804, *Scene From Gil Blas*, and thereafter he painted only portraits. He was sometimes called an 'English Rembrandt' and 'the Cornish Caravaggio'.

In his last years he lectured at the British Institution and the Royal Academy, his work being published as *Lectures on Painting* (1809) with a memoir by his widow, who was also renowned as a novelist. The final lecture was given on 9 March 1807. By this time he was suffering from 'a disease of the spinal marrow, affecting the brain', and died in London on 6 April 1807. He was buried at St Paul's Cathedral.

John Passmore Edwards

Newspaper Proprietor and Philanthropist

John Passmore Edwards was born on 24 March 1823 at Blackwater, near Truro, second son of William Edwards and his wife Susan Passmore. He was educated at the village school, but left to help his father work as carpenter, brewer, publican and nurseryman, and taught himself from books in his spare time. While working as a clerk for a Truro lawyer in 1843, he became interested in the Anti-Corn Law League, and in 1844 became the Manchester representative of *The Sentinel*, a London weekly newspaper, part of the league's propaganda campaign. The paper's failure left him with large debts, which he paid by lecturing at 1s a time for various temperance societies. Once he was solvent again, in 1845 he settled in London to earn a living by lecturing and journalism.

Interested in political and social reform, he worked tirelessly on behalf of the Early Closing Association, a body which advocated the prohibition of alcohol. He admired the Chartists, but disagreed with their endorsement of violence to achieve their aims. After joining the London Peace Society, he was a delegate to their conferences at Brussels in 1848, Paris in 1849, and Frankfurt in 1850. Later he was active in the Political Reform Association and the Ballot Society, and in 1894 he was appointed president of the London Reform Association, which supported progressive municipal legislation. He endorsed the suppression of gambling and the opium trade, the abolition of capital punishment, flogging in the armed forces, and the newspaper tax. In 1850 he put his savings into a weekly newspaper, *The Public Good*, which he wrote, printed, and published from his room in Paternoster Row. It proved a costly failure, as did several other journals which he launched shortly afterwards, such as *Biographical Magazine*, *Peace Advocate*, and *Poetic Magazine*. The pressure resulted in bankruptcy and a nervous breakdown, but after he recovered he established himself as a freelance journalist and gradually discharged his debts.

In 1862 he purchased the *Building News*, and in 1869 the *Mechanics Magazine*, both of which became successful. In 1876 he purchased *The Echo*, the first halfpenny newspaper, a Conservative-supporting journal, which under his ownership transferred its allegiance to the Liberal cause. He had been parliamentary candidate for Truro in 1868 and was elected Liberal MP for Salisbury in the 1880 election but resigned his seat after two years, saying he had not found the Commons 'such a fruitful field of usefulness as expected'. In 1884 Andrew Carnegie, the Scots-American steel magnate, and Samuel Storey, MP for Sunderland and local newspaper proprietor, bought a two-thirds interest in *The Echo* but Edwards bought back full control in 1886. In 1898 he sold it to a syndicate of Liberal nonconformists, but it closed in 1905.

For some years he had used his profits from *The Echo* to fund a number of philanthropic ventures, mainly to improve social conditions in his native Cornwall and the poorer districts of London. His gifts included over twenty libraries, eight hospitals, five convalescent homes, homes for epileptics, four homes for boys, three art galleries, a museum, many drinking fountains, books and busts of literary worthies to reading rooms and libraries throughout the country, an endowed scholarship to Oxford University, a lifeboat to Dundee, and a public garden to Woolwich. Though he repeatedly declined a knighthood he accepted honorary freedoms of five boroughs, including Liskeard, Falmouth and Truro. He died at his Hampstead home, Netherhall Gardens, on 22 April 1911. The picture shows the Passmore Edwards Institute in Hayle.

Andrew Pears

Founder of Pears Soap

Andrew Pears was born probably in Mevagissey in 1766 or 1767, the son of a farmer. Almost nothing is known of his early years, except that as a young man he was apprenticed to a barber and went to London to establish his own barber's shop in Gerrard Street, where he attracted the custom of many wealthy families, often attending to patrons in their own homes. His shop was used for the manufacture and sale of rouges, powders, creams, dentifrices and other beauty aids, all of which were commonly used by the middle and upper classes of the day in order to protect themselves from or cover up the damage caused by the harsh soaps then in regular use.

The wealthy preferred to cultivate a delicate white complexion, as a tanned face was generally associated with the working classes. Pears was quick to realise that there was a market for a gentler soap to preserve these complexions. Through trial and error he found a way by which he could remove the impurities and developing a formula in which ordinary soap was refined, dissolved in alcohol, distilled, and then shaped into individual bars. The result was a high-quality soap, described as having the delicate perfume of English garden flowers, and probably the first of its kind. It had the additional benefit of being transparent, thus looking more attractive, and making bubbles that lasted longer. He began making and selling this unique product in 1789.

With these qualities, the image of Pears Soap was instantly established for posterity. Its inventor's method of mellowing and ageing each long-lasting Pears Bar for over two months has stood the test of time and been maintained to this day, with natural oils and pure glycerine used, combined with the fragrance of rosemary, cedar and thyme.

It was said that he cared more for the quality of the products that bore his name than the number of people who bought them. Nevertheless the soap was very popular, and inspired numerous inferior imitations from competitors. In order to make the real product readily identifiable, he personally signed the wrapper of each bar as a guarantee of its quality. Though he manufactured other products as well for some years, his 1s and 2s 6d squares of amber soap proved by far the most successful. Because of the high price of his products, the market for them was necessarily an exclusive one, and he had no need to advertise his wares.

In 1835 he established a partnership with his grandson Francis. They moved from Gerrard Street to new premises in the city at 55 Wells Street, just off Oxford Street, and founded the family business as A. & F. Pears. The business continued to remain successful and Andrew retired in 1838, leaving Francis in sole charge. He died on 24 April 1845 at Wells Street, London.

David Penhaligon

Politician

David Charles Penhaligon was born at Truro on 6 June 1944. His father Robert was owner of a caravan park and garage in Truro. He attended Truro School and Cornwall Technical College where he studied mechanical engineering, then joined the Camborne engineering firm Holman Bros in 1962 as a research and development engineer, while studying towards a higher national diploma in engineering at Cornwall Technical College as a Chartered Mechanical Engineer. Although chair of the Cornish Young Liberals from 1966 to 1968, he was not selected as Liberal candidate for Truro in the 1966 general election or for Falmouth and Camborne in 1968, as his strong Cornish accent was thought to place him at a disadvantage.

In the 1970 general election he contested Totnes, coming third. Next year he was selected as candidate for Truro; in the election of February 1974 he sharply reduced the Conservative majority, and in October 1974 he became MP with a margin of 464, making it the only Liberal gain of that election. At Westminster he advocated a national minimum wage and increased state pensions. Despite his interest in national issues his main concerns were local, particularly those of the tin-mining industry and local fishing. He spoke with conviction and knowledge about problems of rural Cornwall with high road-fuel costs and inadequate infrastructure, saying that one needed 'more in an economy than just tourism, ice cream and deckchairs.'

Initially opposed to the Lib-Lab pact in March 1977 which kept a minority Labour government in power, he later changed his mind and told the Liberal Assembly in September 1977 that it had achieved an 'economic revolution'. At a special assembly in January 1978 he urged delegates representing Liberal members to continue the pact. He thought an early general election would be bad for the party, particularly in view of a scandal over previous leader Jeremy Thorpe, recently charged with conspiracy to murder. Penhaligon had urged Thorpe to stand down, and refused to help his campaign when Thorpe unsuccessfully sought re-election.

In the 1979 election he kept his seat with a greatly increased majority of 8,708. According to the *Guardian* during the campaign, 'When he catches the train to Paddington, he is a Cornish rebel going to battle in an alien land, not a carpetbagger going home.' During the first years of the new Conservative government he strongly opposed nuclear power, but unlike most Liberal Party members he supported NATO and nuclear weapons, describing a separate European non-nuclear defence as 'akin to behaving like a virgin in a brothel', while endorsing demands for dual key control of US cruise missiles based in Britain.

In 1981 he supported the SDP-Liberal Alliance, although he resented SDP attempts to take control of the Liberal Party's target seats. In the 1983 election his majority of 10,480 made his the safest Liberal/SDP Alliance seat in the country. He argued for a merger between the SDP and the Liberals under a single leader, and headed the Liberal by-election unit which planned the campaigns in individual seats. At the Liberal Assembly in September 1984 he became the first sitting MP to be elected President of the Liberal Party. In November 1986 he was one of three MPs who each took over the Jimmy Young show on BBC Radio 2 for a week.

Widely admired and liked across the political spectrum for his affable personality and good humour, he was seen as a future Liberal leader, and was to receive the OBE for political services in the 1987 New Year's Honours List. Tragically he was killed in a car crash early in the morning of 22 December 1986 while going to visit members of the workforce at St Austell's post office.

Dolly Pentreath

Last Cornish Speaker

Dolly Pentreath was born between 1670 and 1700 and lived in the parish of Paul, next to Mousehole. Brought up as a Cornish speaker, she learnt only to speak English as an adult. Her husband was a fisherman and she sold fish, smoked her pipe, drank flagons of beer and spoke 'proper old Cornish'. Rumour had it that she was also a witch.

She is often considered to be the last monoglot speaker of the Cornish language, the last person who spoke only Cornish and not English, a legend which arose as a result of an account written by Daines Barrington, a visitor to Cornwall who discovered and interviewed Dolly and some other Cornish speakers in Mousehole at a time when everyone thought the language had died. She has passed into legend for cursing at people with a long stream of fierce Cornish whenever she became angry. One story still told about her is the one saying that when a press-gang landed in search of men for the navy, she picked up a hatchet and fought them back to their boats, cursing them in old Cornish so violently that the crew never dared to return.

On another occasion she saved a man from being hanged. He had escaped from the courtroom after sentence of death and burst into her house overlooking the quay, desperate for refuge. She promptly ordered him to hide in the chimney, where there was a cavity large enough for a man to stand upright. By the time the officer and his men had arrived in the kitchen, she was sitting on a stool, bare-legged with her feet over a tub of water. When they asked her if she had seen a man on the premises, she dismissed the suggestion that she would admit anyone while she was washing her feet. She let them search her house, and when they failed to find anyone, she chased them away with a torrent of invective, wielding an axe as she did so. After they had gone, she put the man on a fishing boat bound for Guernsey, a ready place of hiding for those on the run from the law.

A room still exists in the Keigwin Arms in which she enjoyed a regular pint of beer and her pipe, as well as looking out of the window to shout at the fishermen when they landed. Bargains never escaped her eye, and she would walk into Penzance with her wicker basket on her back, always prepared to haggle and never taking no for an answer.

She died in December 1777, aged 102 according to some sources. Though some scholars have named other Cornish speakers who outlived her and therefore question any claim that she was the last true speaker of the language, popular history recognises her passing as essentially marking the death of Cornish as a community language. Her last words were said to have been '*Me ne vidn cewsel Sawznek!*' ('I don't want to speak English!'). After she was buried in the parish churchyard of Paul a monument to her (pictured), set in the churchyard wall, was erected in 1860 jointly by Louis Lucien Bonaparte and the then vicar of Paul, the Revd John Garret. Cut in stone is a transcription of the Fifth Commandment, 'Honour thy father and thy mother' in old Cornish. The monument was allegedly placed over the wrong grave in 1860 and was moved to its current location in 1882.

Rosamunde Pilcher

Author

Rosamunde Scott was born in Lelant on 22 September 1924, and attended St Clare's, Polwithen and Howell's School, Llandaff, before going to secretarial college. She began writing for her own amusement when she was seven, and published her first short story at the age of eighteen. From 1943 to 1946 she served with the Women's Royal Naval Service. In December 1946 she married Graham Hope Pilcher and they moved to Dundee, where she embarked on a literary career by writing short stories and love stories for women's magazines.

She then decided to take up full-length fiction. In 1949 her first book, *Half-Way to the Moon*, was published by Mills and Boon under the pseudonym Jane Fraser.

Another ten novels followed under the same alias, including *Dangerous Intruder* (1951), *A Family Affair* (1958), and the last, *The Keeper's House* (1963). In later years she dismissed them as 'frightfully wet little novels – romantic stuff with red roses on the cover'. Her first novel written as Rosamunde Pilcher, *A Secret to Tell*, was published in 1955. Many of her stories was set in the fictional Cornish town of Porthkerris, a fictional name for St Ives, where she had spent much of her childhood.

By 1965 she had abandoned the pseudonym and was using her own name for all of her output. The novel which really established her and, in her words, 'changed her life', was *The Shell Seekers*. A family saga set in London and Cornwall between the Second World War and the present, it was published in 1987 and became a major success in Britain and America, where it topped the New York Times bestseller list. It sold more than 5 million copies worldwide and was adapted for the stage by Terence Brady and Charlotte Bingham.

Her subsequent titles, including *September* (1990), *Coming Home* (1995) and *The Key* (1996), made her one of the most successful contemporary female authors in Britain. Several of them were filmed for television, mainly on location in Cornwall. *Coming Home* (1998), starring Peter O'Toole and Joanna Lumley, was shot in Lelant, Prideaux Place, Marazion and Penzance, and a year later its sequel *Nancherrow*, with Susan Hampshire and Patrick Macnee, was filmed in Chapel Porth, Wheal Coates, Towan Head, Newquay, Bodmin and Wenford Railway. Many of her stories were adapted for television in Germany, where her books had always been especially popular. In the words of one critic they 'comfortably occupied that undervalued middle ground between light fiction and serious literature'.

She retired from writing in 2000 after the publication of *Winter Solstice*, by which time she had written nineteen full-length novels under her own name, in addition to two volumes of short stories. Two years later she was awarded the OBE. In an interview in 2004, shortly before her eightieth birthday, she said that 'to be a successful writer you have to touch people, you have to make people want to turn the page'.

St Piran

Patron Saint of Cornwall

St Piran or Perran was an early sixth-century Cornish abbot and saint, believed to be of Irish origin. He is regarded as the patron saint of Cornwall (although St Michael and St Petroc also have some claim to this title) and the patron saint of tin miners. His flag is a white cross on a black background.

According to legend, the heathen Irish tied him to a millstone and rolled it over the edge of a cliff into a stormy sea. The waters immediately became calm, and he floated away, landing upon the sandy beach of Perranzabuloe. There he was soon joined by a number of his Christian converts, and between them they went on to found the Abbey of Lanpiran, with Piran becoming the abbot. Tin had been smelted in Cornwall since before the arrival of the Romans, but their skills had long since been lost. He rediscovered the technique when his black hearthstone, which was probably a slab of tin-bearing ore, had the tin smelt out of it and rose to the top in the form of a white cross, hence the image used on his flag ever since.

By around the thirteenth century he had become identified with the Irish Saint Ciarán of Saighir, who founded the monastery at Seirkieran (Saighir) in County Offaly. The fourteenth-century chronicle of the *Life of St Piran*, probably written at Exeter Cathedral, is a complete copy of an earlier Irish life of Saint Ciarán of Saighir, although with different parentage and a different ending that takes into account Piran's works in Cornwall, and especially details of his death and the movements of his Cornish shrine.

St Piran's Day is celebrated on 5 March. It has long been a popular Cornish festival, and the term 'Perrantide' was coined to describe the week leading up to 5 March, with a number of Cornish-themed events taking place in the Duchy and in areas elsewhere which have a large community descended from Cornish emigrants. The foremost St Piran's Day event is a march across the dunes to St Piran's Cross which many attend, generally dressed in black, white and gold, and carrying the Cornish flag. A play based on the life of St Piran, in Cornish, has been enacted in recent years as part of the event. Daffodils are carried and placed at the cross, and also feature in celebrations in Truro, probably due to their 'gold' colour.

The fifth March is the traditional feast day of St Ciarán of Saighir as well as St Piran, though the Calendar of Launceston Church records an alternative date of 18 November for the latter. At his death, it was said, the remains of the Blessed Martin the Abbot which he had brought from Ireland were buried with him at Perranzabuloe. His own remains were exhumed at a later date and redistributed to be venerated in various reliquaries. St Piran's Old Church, Perranzabuloe, had a reliquary containing his head and also a hearse in which his body was placed for processionals, while Exeter Cathedral apparently has one of his arms.

William Pryce

Surgeon, Mineralogist and Antiquary

William Pryce was born at Redruth, where he was baptised on 14 June 1735. He was the only son of surgeon Samuel Pryce and his wife, Catherine, a niece of the antiquary William Borlase (q.v.). A sister died in infancy, he was orphaned at an early age, and brought up by the prominent Falmouth attorney Philip Webber, a distant relation who became a lifelong friend.

In 1751 he was apprenticed to Philip Tingcombe, a surgeon in Redruth. After studying dissection under Dr Hunter, thought to be either John or William Hunter of London, he established his own practice in the town. In August 1758 he married Catherine Michell and they had two sons, Samuel, who became a surgeon and banker, and William, a surgeon, as well as a daughter who died in infancy.

He had commercial interests in local mining, bought shares in local mines, and managed some small-scale mining operations. Aware of the advantages to be gained from bringing coal more cheaply to the local tin and copper mines, he developed a scheme to build a quay at Portreath in 1763, but did then found he had insufficient finance for such an ambitious venture. When his financial problems became acute soon afterwards, he had to sell his shares.

After being encouraged by Borlase to make the best use of his knowledge, he turned his back on speculative ventures in order to concentrate more fully on scholarship and produce a book on the history of mining. He studied several manuscripts on the history of mining in Cornwall, and added information which he had obtained from his own observations and from local experts, as well as from others including William Cookworthy, the mineralogist and 'father of English porcelain', and engineer Matthew Boulton. The result, *Mineralogia Cornubiensis*, was published by subscription in 1778.

His contribution to the literature of mineralogy was recognised when he was awarded an MD by St Andrews University in 1781, and elected as a Fellow of the Society of Antiquaries two years later. The society's Vice-President, Barrington Daines, knew that Pryce had access to important Cornish manuscripts by the antiquaries Thomas Tonkin (q.v.) and William Hals, and encouraged him in the plans he had had for a while to compile and publish a Cornish grammar and dictionary. *Archaeologia Cornu-Britannica*, which appeared in 1790, was in effect based largely on collating the manuscripts of Tonkin, Hals and others, though he made use of his own researches by adding information obtained through interviews with elderly people who claimed to speak Cornish. Although he took care to credit himself as editor of the work rather than author, and acknowledging his sources in the work's preface, some accusations of plagiarism were levelled against him, and it was felt that he had relied too heavily on the work of others.

He died in December 1790 at Redruth, where he was buried on the twentieth of the month.

Sir Arthur Quiller-Couch

Author

Sir Arthur Thomas Quiller-Couch was born in Bodmin on 21 November 1863, grandson of the famous botanist Jonathan Couch (q.v.). He was educated at Newton Abbot College, Clifton College, and Trinity College, Oxford where he became a lecturer after obtaining a classics degree. While there he published several novels under the pseudonym 'Q', including *Dead Man's Rock* (1887), *Troy Town* (1888) and *The Splendid Spur* (1889). His father had died in 1884 and his family were not very well off, so his first novels were a way of helping to support his family while he was still at Oxford. *Troy Town*, a farce set in Fowey, was the most successful of these early novels.

He spent some time as a journalist in London, mainly as a contributor to the *Speaker*, before returning to Cornwall in 1891, and settling in Fowey the following year. His fascination with Fowey had begun in 1879 when he was only sixteen, the association continued the rest of his life, and there he met his future wife. As well as publishing a series of critical articles, he completed Robert Louis Stevenson's unfinished novel *St Ives*. He published in 1896 a series of critical articles, *Adventures in Criticism*. He was also known as a poet; his poetical work is contained in *Poems and Ballads* (1896); and compiler of anthologies, his anthology from the sixteenth and seventeenth-century English lyricists, *The Golden Pomp* (1895), and the *Oxford Book of English Verse, 1250-1900* (1900).

He was knighted in 1910, and two years later he was appointed Professor of English Literature at Cambridge University, where he oversaw the beginnings of the English faculty. As a literary critic, his commentaries on the subject included *Studies in Literature* (1918) and *On the Art of Reading* (1920). Later he edited the *Oxford Book of English Prose* (1923), the thirty-volume work of fiction *Tales and Romances* (1928-9), and in collaboration with John Dover Wilson, several volumes of *The New Shakespeare*, published by the Cambridge University Press.

He was an active worker in local politics for the Liberal party, Commodore of the Royal Fowey Yacht Club from 1911 until his death, helped in the Restoration of the Charter of the Borough of Fowey and the revival of the town council. He was a member of Cornwall County Council's Education Committee and a magistrate, and was given the freedom of Fowey, Bodmin and Truro. He was made a Bard at the Cornish Gorsedd in 1928, taking the Bardic name Marghak Cough (Red Knight).

He continued to write novels throughout his life; later titles including *The Roll Call of Honour* (1927), *From a Cornish Window* (1928), and *The Splendid Spur* (1937). Many of his fictional works have been neglected for some years, but contain a wealth of Cornish folklore. He died on 12 May 1944, leaving an unfinished autobiography *Memories and Opinions*, published the following year. His unfinished novel *Castle Dor*, a version of *Tristan and Isolde*, set in nineteenth-century Cornwall, was later completed by Daphne du Maurier at the request of his daughter Foy and published in 1962. A memorial to him is situated at the top of Penleath Point at the entrance to Pont Creek, Fowey.

Philip Rashleigh

Mineralogist and Antiquary

Philip Rashleigh was born on 28 December 1729 at Aldermanbury, London, the eldest son of Jonathan Rashleigh, a London merchant, MP and Cornish landowner. He was educated at Oxford University, but did not get a degree. Members of his family had long been owners of estates throughout Cornwall, and several of his forbears had represented Fowey in Parliament. On the death of his father he was elected member for Fowey in 1765 and sat continuously until retiring in 1802, becoming Father of the House. Nevertheless he spent most of his time in Cornwall, rarely attended the House of Commons, and even when he did was an infrequent speaker.

Developments in tin and copper mining during the eighteenth century led him to develop a lifelong interest in mineralogy. Soon after he inherited the family estates he began to form a collection of minerals, acquiring specimens from local miners and mine owners, as well as purchasing and exchanging examples with mineral dealers, collectors and mineralogists at home and abroad. The exploitation of the upper zones of the rich Cornwall deposits enabled him to obtain many unusual and rare minerals, and he was one of the first to compile detailed catalogues of the source and locality of each specimen.

By 1794 he had acquired over 4,000 mineral specimens, and chose Henry Bone (q.v.) to produce paintings for hand-coloured engravings showing 194 specimens. The first volume was published in 1797 as *Specimens of British Minerals, Selected from the Cabinet of Philip Rashleigh*. A second volume followed in 1802, with twenty-one plates illustrating forty-eight specimens by artists including his sister Rachel, watercolourist and geologist Thomas Richard Underwood, and engraver Thomas Medland. He thus became the first man in Britain to publish a book including accurate coloured illustrations of minerals. Paintings for a third volume were prepared by Harriet Rashleigh and James Sowerby, but remained unpublished at the time of his death. The financial crisis engendered by the war with France and subsequent increase in prices, as well as intense competition from other collectors, sharply curtailed his activities, but he continued to purchase further specimens until within two or three years of his death.

As an enthusiastic collector of antiquities, with a particular interest in pieces obtained from tin streamworks associated with the early days of Cornish mining, one of his most treasured acquisitions was a late Saxon hoard of metalwork from Trewhiddle, later acquired by the British Museum.

He made his home at the sixteenth-century mansion of Menabilly, near Fowey, which was later the inspiration for Manderley in Daphne du Maurier's (q.v.) *Rebecca*, and dedicated a room there to his collections. He published several papers in *Archaeologia*, and in recognition of the value of his research into and knowledge of Cornish minerals he was elected to the Royal Society and to the Society of Antiquaries in 1788.

In 1782 he married his first cousin, Jane Pole. He died at Menabilly on 26 June 1811 and was buried at Tywardreath. As he and his wife left no children, his mineral collection and the original paintings of his minerals were bequeathed to his nephew, William, and remained at Menabilly until 1902. Most of them were later acquired by the Museum of the Royal Institution of Cornwall and the Natural History Museum.

Cyrus Redding

Journalist and Author

Cyrus Redding was born probably at Truro on 2 February 1785, the son of Robert Redding, a Baptist minister at Falmouth and later Truro, and his wife Joanna. One of his earliest memories, which remained with him throughout his life, was seeing John Wesley standing on a pile of Norway timber to preach at Falmouth Quay. Educated mainly at home by his father, and then at Truro grammar school, he had a volume of poetry printed at his own expense.

After settling in London during his early twenties, he worked as a journalist. His first post was as a staff writer for *The Pilot*, a newly-founded paper concerned with East Indian affairs. A year or two later he returned to the westcountry and became editor of the weekly *Plymouth Chronicle*. In June 1810 he became founder editor of the *West Briton and Cornwall Advertiser*. In 1812 he married Julia Ann Moyle, and they had two daughters.

In 1814 he went to France for several years, settling mainly in Paris, where he edited Galignani's *Messenger*, a Parisian daily newspaper published in English, from 1815 to 1818. In 1815 he also wrote the Paris correspondence for the *London Examiner* and proudly delivered to English correspondents what was regarded as the greatest journalistic scoop of its time, the breaking news of Napoleon's defeat at Waterloo in June 1815. From 1821 to 1830 he was working as the editor of and regular contributor to the *New Monthly Magazine*, started under the nominal editorship of the poet Thomas Campbell. From 1831 to 1833 he edited, again in conjunction with Campbell, *The Metropolitan*, a monthly journal of literature, science and art, but it did not prove a success. For a while he also edited in succession the *Bath Guardian* and the *Staffordshire Examiner*. In 1841 he started two short-lived ventures, the *English Journal* and the *London Journal*.

After these failures in the world of journalism, he relinquished newspaper editorship in favour of writing books. His most successful work was a *History and Description of Modern Wines* (1833), which went into several editions, advocated a reduction in the duties on French wines, and did much to advocate a reduction on the wine tariff in 1860. His *Gabrielle: a Tale of the Swiss Mountains* (1829), and his *Shipwrecks and Disasters at Sea* (1833), for younger readers, both sold well. He produced *An Illustrated Itinerary of the County of Cornwall* (1842), which had been planned as the first title in a large series of county histories, though he only published one further volume, on Lancashire. A versatile writer, he was also responsible for several other works of fiction, including *Keeping up Appearances* (1861), and *A Wife and Not a Wife* (1867), in addition to various works of biography, memoirs, travel and poetry.

During his career he came into contact with many worthies, including William Beckford, of whom he wrote a memoir in 1859, and John Wilson, acting editor of *Blackwood's Magazine* from 1817 to 1854. In his three-volume autobiography, *Fifty Years' Recollections, Literary and Personal, with Observations on Men and Things* (1858), he wrote about his friendship with contemporaries including Daniel O'Connell, Mme de Stael, J.M.W. Turner, and August von Schlegel, Professor of Literature at Bonn. He died at his home in Hill Road, St John's Wood, London on 28 May 1870, and was buried at Willesden cemetery.

Rick Rescorla

United States Army Officer

Cyril Richard Rescorla was born on 27 May 1939 in Hayle. In 1943 the town was host to the 175th Infantry Regiment of the US 29th Infantry Division, preparing for the invasion of Nazi-occupied Europe, and as a boy he was fascinated by the sight of the troops.

He joined the army in 1957, became a paratrooper with the Parachute Regiment, served with an intelligence unit in Cyprus, and as a paramilitary police inspector in the Northern Rhodesia Police. After returning to London and civilian life, he served briefly with the Metropolitan Police Service, then joined the American army, undertook basic training at Fort Dix, New Jersey, then attended Officer Candidate School and airborne training at Fort Benning, Georgia. On graduation he was assigned as a platoon leader in the 2nd Battalion, 7th Cavalry Regiment, 1st Cavalry Division (Airmobile). In Vietnam he took part in the battle of Ia Drang in 1965 and was awarded the Silver Star, the Bronze Star with Oak Leaf Cluster, a Purple Heart, and the Vietnamese Cross of Gallantry.

Becoming an American citizen in 1968, he was awarded BA and MA degrees in Literature at the University of Oklahoma. Moving to South Carolina, he taught criminal justice at the University of South Carolina for three years and published a textbook on the subject. He served in the United States Army Reserve till 1990, retiring as a colonel. In 1985 he joined the financial services firm Dean Witter as their security director. When the organisation merged with Morgan Stanley in 1997, he became the company's director of security in the World Trade Center. After his first marriage ended in divorce, prostate cancer was diagnosed but later went into remission. In 1999 he married Susan Greer, after a courtship which included singing her the Cornish ballad, *The White Rose*, and sending her white roses each week until he proposed.

Some years previously he had warned the Port Authority, owner of the World Trade Center, that the building was vulnerable to terrorist attacks, and recommended to senior management at Morgan Stanley that the company should leave the premises. Although little consideration was given to his words, he was at least able to insist that all employees, including senior executives, should practise emergency evacuations every three months.

When American Airlines Flight 11 struck World Trade Center Tower 1 on 11 September 2001 at 8.46 a.m. he ignored official advice to stay put and began the orderly evacuation of Morgan Stanley's 2,700 employees on twenty floors of World Trade Center Tower 2, and 1,000 employees in WTC 5. Most of them were safely out of the buildings by the time United Airlines Flight 175 hit WTC 2 at 9.02 a.m. After leading many to safety, he returned to the building to rescue others still inside. When a colleague tried to persuade him to leave the building, he replied he would when everyone else was out. He was seen as high as the seventy-second floor evacuating people, clearing the floors and working his way down, and last noticed heading up the stairs of the tenth floor of the collapsing WTC 2. His body was never recovered. Thanks to his bravery, only six Morgan Stanley employees were killed, including him and three of his deputies. A memorial stone was erected to him at Hayle, and in 2003 he was posthumously awarded the White Cross of Cornwall by the Cornish Stannary Parliament.

Jeff Rowe ('Jethro')

Comedian

Jeff Rowe was born in 1948 in St Buryan. After leaving school he was apprenticed as a carpenter and then worked as a timberman in the tin mines. At the age of eighteen he joined the St Just and District Operatic Society, singing bass voice. While performing in pubs in and around Cornwall, one night his voice suddenly failed him. For want of an alternative, he started telling jokes instead, and in his words 'things progressed from there really.' The jokes gradually took over from the singing, and soon he was being hailed as Cornwall's top comic. In an interview some years later, he paid tribute to his idols Arthur Lowe and John Le Mesurier of *Dad's Army*, and stand-up comics Les Dawson and Frank Carson, whom he said had been his main inspiration.

In addition to his appearances on stage and video, he became a regular guest on Des O'Connor's television shows, starting with a spot on the *Des O'Connor Tonight* show in 1990, followed by a return for the Christmas Eve programme later that year. It was the first time that a comedian had been invited back during one series. He also appeared five times on Jim Davidson's *Generation Game* show, twice giving a demonstration of how to make a Cornish pasty. He was also involved in one of the show's longest sequences of out-takes, removed due to his and Davidson's uncontrolled mirth but later shown separately. Davidson said that he regarded Jethro as his favourite storyteller, one of his great stories being 'Train don't stop Camborne Wednesdays'.

In March 1995 he walked around 100 miles from Land's End to his home town of Lewdown in order to raise money for the Bristol Cancer Open Scanner Appeal. On the way he gave a show each night at a local venue, and raised £20,000 altogether.

He has hosted two shows of his own, *The Jethro Junction*, on HTV, and recorded several videos and DVDs. In December 2001 he took part in the *Royal Variety Show*. His great loves are his horses which he shows all over the country and with whom he has won several major prizes. He also has his own venue at Lewdown, Jethro's Club, where he gives a performance each year for charity.

A.L. Rowse

Historian

Alfred Leslie Rowse was born in Tregonissey near St Austell on 4 December 1903, the son of Richard Rowse, a china-clay worker, and his wife Annie. He won a place at St Austell Grammar School, now Poltair School, and then a scholarship to Christ Church, Oxford in 1921 where he read history, graduated with first class honours, was elected a Fellow of All Souls College in 1925, and awarded an MA in 1929. In 1927 he was appointed lecturer at Merton College, where he stayed until 1930. In 1931 and 1935 he unsuccessfully contested the parliamentary seat of Penryn and Falmouth as a Labour candidate. He condemned the National Government's policy of appeasement in the 1930s and the economic and political consequences for Great Britain of fighting a second war with Germany. In later years he moved increasingly towards the political right, developing a reputation for irascibility and deploring the lowering of standards in modern society, reportedly saying: 'This filthy twentieth century. I hate its guts'.

A prolific author, he published around 100 books, as well as articles in newspapers and magazines in Britain and America. His first book *On History, A Study of Present Tendencies* (1927) was the seventh volume of Kegan Paul's *Psyche Miniature General Series*. In 1935 he co-edited Charles Henderson's *Essays in Cornish History*. His other Cornish titles included *Tudor Cornwall* (1941), the memoir *A Cornish Childhood* (1942), probably his most successful title, and *The Little Land of Cornwall* (1986).

Always fascinated by the Tudor era, he made his mark with his first full-length historical monograph, the biography, *Sir Richard Grenville of the Revenge* (1937). A trilogy comprising *The Elizabethan Age: The England of Elizabeth* (1950), *The Expansion of Elizabethan England* (1955), and *The Elizabethan Renaissance* (1971-72), dealing with late sixteenth-century English society and culture, is often considered his most important work. A biography *Shakespeare* (1963) was followed by a second, *Shakespeare the Man* (1973), and he returned to the subject in his last book, *My View of Shakespeare* (1996). His prolific output also included biographies of English historical and literary figures such as John Milton, Christopher Marlowe and Sir Arthur Quiller-Couch (q.v.). A devoted cat lover, he also wrote biographies of several of his feline friends, including Peter the white cat of Trenarren. His short stories were mainly about Cornwall, as was his poetry, to be found in *Collected Poems* (1981), and he wrote on the subject of human sexuality in his controversial *Homosexuals In History* (1977).

After delivering the British Academy's 1957 Raleigh Lecture on History about Sir Richard Grenville's place in English history he became a Fellow of the Academy in 1958. Among the honours he was awarded were Fellowship of the Royal Historical Society, an honorary D. Litt by the University of Exeter and a DCL by the University of New Brunswick, Fredericton, Canada, in 1960. In 1968 he was made a Bard of Cornish Gorsedd, taking the bardic name Lef A Gernow (Voice of Cornwall) which reflected his high standing in the Cornish community. In 1997 he was made a Companion of Honour.

He retired from Oxford in 1973 to Trenarren House, where he died on 3 October 1997, having bequeathed his book collection including many first editions and personal archive of manuscripts, diaries, and correspondence to Exeter University. His ashes were buried in the Campdowns Cemetery, Charlestown.

Kristin Scott Thomas

Actress

Kristin Scott Thomas was born in Redruth on 24 May 1960. The eldest of five children, she is the elder sister of actress Serena Scott Thomas, the niece of Admiral Sir Richard Thomas, a former Black Rod in the House of Lords, and a great-niece of Captain Scott, who perished in the Antarctic in 1912. Her father, a Royal Navy pilot, died in a flying accident in 1964. In her early childhood the family moved to Dorset, and her mother married another Royal Navy pilot, who by tragic coincidence also died in a flying accident in 1970.

She was educated at Cheltenham Ladies' College, which she disliked as she felt she was not academic enough and less glamorous than her younger sister, and St Antony's Leweston School for Girls. Later she attended a course to become a drama teacher in London, where her efforts to transfer to become an actress were rebuffed when she was told she would never be good enough. At the age of nineeen she left to work as an au pair for a family in Paris, then then studied acting at the École nationale supérieure des arts et techniques du théâtre (ENSATT) in Paris.

On graduation she was cast opposite pop star Prince as a French girl in *Under the Cherry Moon* (1986). Although the film was not a box-office success, her acting brought her to the notice of a wider audience. Her first major success was in 1994 when she played opposite Hugh Grant in *Four Weddings And A Funeral*, saying, 'I love it that people still think of it – that film is going to be around a very long time'. It won her a BAFTA film award for best actress in a supporting role. Some years later she said in an interview that the parts in which she had been most successful were those she had most desperately wanted, one of them being that of Fiona in *Four Weddings*. 'I couldn't think of anyone better for that part than me. And the other was *The English Patient*. Occasionally, you read scripts and, well, there you are on the page.'

She also appeared briefly with Tom Cruise in *Mission: Impossible* and played the unfaithful wife in *The English Patient*, both in 1996. A year later she was chosen by *People* magazine as one of the fifty 'Most Beautiful People in the World'. Her subsequent films included *The Horse Whisperer* (1998), *Random Hearts* (1999), *Up at the Villa* (2000), *Gosford Park* (2001), and *The Other Boleyn Girl* (2008). A fluent French speaker since she was young, she has overdubbed herself in French in some pictures.

She married French gynaecologist François Olivennes in 1981, from whom she was later separated, and they had three children, Hannah, Joseph and Georges. She was awarded the OBE in 2003, and the Légion d'honneur by the French government in 2005. Although the majority of her career has been in the cinema, she has also appeared on stage and television. In London's West End she appeared in *Three Sisters* (2004), *As You Desire Me* (2006), and *The Seagull* (2007), in which she played the female lead, Irina Arkadina, and as a result of which she was awarded the Best Actress prize in the Laurence Olivier awards in March 2008. Her television roles included drama as well as brief appearances in the situation comedy *Absolutely Fabulous* and the motoring programme *Top Gear*.

Tim Smit

Chief Executive and Founder of the Eden Project

Tim Smit was born in Scheveningen, Holland on 25 September 1954, educated at Vinehall and Cranbrook School, Kent, then read archaeology and anthropology at Durham University, and subsequently worked as an archaeologist for two years in the North East of England. At first he worked in the music business as a songwriter, arranger and producer with acts including Barry Manilow, the Nolan Sisters and Louise Tucker, in the course of which he was awarded seven platinum and gold discs. Nevertheless he later said that his greatest contribution to music was to 'do a Captain Oates and leave'.

In 1987 he and his family moved to Cornwall, where his interest in science and natural history took over. Three years later he formed a team to research and restore the then-derelict 'lost gardens of Heligan', of twelfth-century origin, at Pentewan, near St Austell, to their former glory. They were opened to the public at Easter 1992, and with an estimated average 350,000 visitors a year, they rapidly became one of the county's top tourist attractions. In 1997 they became the subject of a six-part Channel 4 TV documentary.

A few years later he became one of the driving forces behind the Eden Project, near St Austell, an £80 million initiative to build three transparent biomes, or hexagonal eco-bubbles which were massive greenhouses, in an old china-clay pit. By bringing the idea to reality, Smit and his board intended to educate people about environmental matters, and encourage a greater understanding with such concerns. His chief role from the start was to raise the necessary funds, while leaving the site design to architect Nicholas Grimshaw. Each biome contained different eco-climates loosely based on the widely diverging climates to be found throughout the world, namely tropical jungle, temperate, and desert. One, the Humid Tropics Biome, was the largest greenhouse in the world, covering an area of nearly four acres. The result became what Smit called 'a living theatre of plants', about 250,000 in all. His mission, the man sometimes dubbed the Richard Branson of Cornwall has said, was to change the world into one where 'plants provide a canvas on which we can paint an optimistic future.'

He was awarded an honorary CBE in the New Year honours list of 2002. Four years later he received an honorary Doctor of Design degree from the University of the West of England 'in recognition of his outstanding achievements in promoting the understanding and practice of the responsible management of the vital relationship between plants, people and resources, which have made a major contribution regionally, nationally and internationally to sustainable development, tourism, architecture and landscape architecture'.

Howard Spring

Author

Robert Howard Spring was born in Cardiff, South Wales on 10 February 1889. His father, William Spring, an itinerant gardener from County Cork, and his mother Mary lived in poverty with their nine children in a small two-bedroomed house. His father died while he was still at school and at the age of twelve he started work as an errand boy for a greengrocer, then as office boy with a firm of chartered accountants in Cardiff Docks, before joining the *South Wales Daily News* as a messenger boy. Keen to train as a reporter, he spent his leisure time learning shorthand and taking evening classes at the local university where he studied English, French, Latin, mathematics and history. He became a reporter on both morning and evening editions of the paper.

After his first novel was rejected he began writing short stories. In 1911 he joined the *Yorkshire Observer* in Bradford as a book reviewer before moving in 1915 to the *Manchester Guardian*, as a reporter, but there were only a few months until he was called up for the Army Service Corps as a shorthand typist, being unfit for active service. He held every rank up to and including that of warrant officer, mainly attached to the Intelligence Department. After the war he returned to the *Guardian*, and spent some time in Ireland reporting on the troubles between Great Britain and Sinn Fein.

In 1920 he married Marion Pye, and she introduced him to Cornwall where she had spent her childhood holidays. By 1931 his work had been noticed nationally and he was invited to become book reviewer for the *Evening Standard*. His first published book, *Darkie and Co*, had been written for his children and he had sold all rights in it for £50. Reviewing new books gave him confidence to try writing another novel and his first, *Shabby Tiger* (1934), set in Manchester, was successful enough to encourage him to write a sequel, *Rachel Rosing* (1935). He first achieved major success with *O Absalom!* (1938), his first novel set in Cornwall. Renamed *My Son, My Son!* for the American market, the title was later adopted in Britain as well. *Fame is the Spur* (1940) was also critically acclaimed, and film rights to both titles were sold.

By then he had given up journalism. In 1939 he and Marion moved to Mylor where he became a full-time writer. He adopted a routine of working five mornings a week, writing about 1,000 words in a session, and rarely needing to make major revision to his drafts. *Hard Facts* (1944) and *Dunkerleys* (1946) followed and in 1947 they moved to Falmouth, where he published further titles including *There is No Armour* (1948), *A Sunset Touch* (1953), *These Lovers Fled Away* (1955), *Time and the Hour* (1957), and *I Met a Lady* (1961). He also produced three volumes of autobiography: *Heaven Lies About Us, A Fragment of Infancy* (1939), *In the Meantime* (1942), and *And Another Thing* (1946), later published in one volume.

For a time he was President of the Royal Cornwall Polytechnic Society, Director of the Falmouth School of Art and President of the Cornish Drama League, and he reviewed books for *Country Life*. After a minor stroke he lost the use of his right hand, and recovered enough to write a last novel, *Winds of the Day* (1964). He died following a further stroke at his home on 3 May 1965.

Derek Tangye

Author

Derek Alan Trevithick Tangye was born in London on 29 February 1912. His family had come from Cornwall, where his father practised as a lawyer, and he often spent childhood holidays at the family home at Glendorgal, near Newquay. He was educated at Harrow, then went to work as a clerk in the City and then in Fleet Street as a reporter and gossip writer for the *Daily Express*, *Daily Mail* and *Daily Mirror*. During the war he was employed on special duties at the War Office, and also published his first three books, *Time was Mine* (1941), *Went the Day Well* (1942) and *One King* (1944).

In 1943 he married Jeannie Nicol, who had been an agony aunt on the *Daily Mirror* under the pseudonym of Dorothy Dix, and had been press officer and later head of public relations for the Savoy Hotel Group, which inspired her book *Meet Me at the Savoy*, published under her maiden name Jean Nicol.

In 1949, to the astonishment of friends and colleagues, they left London to settle in Cornwall. When they moved into Minack, or Dorminack, near Lamorna Cove, a small house a mile down a bumpy muddy track, it had an earth floor, but neither water nor electricity. It was a stark contrast with the life to which they had been used, but they found comfort in their escape from the rat race, in being closer to nature and the landscape, in working on a flower farm, and above all in the company of their animals and birds.

The first of over twenty books about this rural idyll, known as the *Minack Chronicles*, *A Gull on the Roof*, was published in 1961. *A Drake at the Door* (1963) was named after a pet Muscovy duck whom they named Boris (after the author Pasternak), and *A Donkey in the Meadow* (1965) after Fred, a donkey whom they rescued from the knacker's yard. Jeannie illustrated the books, which proved very successful. Their simple literary style had tremendous appeal for readers who dreamed of escaping urban and suburban drudgery, and many admirers came from considerable distances to visit them.

Derek and Jeannie adored cats, and one book, *Monty's Leap* (1993), told the story of a ginger tom kitten which had been given to her at the Savoy and came with them to Cornwall. They had named the little stream Monty's Leap, as a symbol for all those who took the decision to change the course of their lives, mirroring the leap forward they took when they left London. Jeannie also wrote four books while at Minack, about life in the hotels she worked in before their marriage. They still returned once or twice a year to London staying in a luxurious suite at the Savoy or at Claridges.

After Jeannie died in 1986, Derek rarely left Cornwall. His book about her, *Jeannie* (1986), also part of the *Minack Chronicles*, was considered by some to be his best. They had already bought several acres of meadow sloping down to the sea, looking out towards St Michael's Mount, and when she was dying they decided to form it into a trust, the Minack Chronicles Trust, as a small haven for solitude and natural life. Increasingly crippled by arthritis and gout, he died on 26 October 1996. John le Carré (q.v.) gave an address at his funeral.

D.M. Thomas

Author

Donald Michael Thomas was born at Carnkie, near Redruth, in 1935, son of a plasterer who built the bungalow in which the family lived for the first four years of his life. It was the part of England, he later recalled, as 'the sadly haunting, wrecked tin-mining area of West Cornwall, its symbol the square ugly granite harmony-filled Wesleyan chapel'. In 1949 he emigrated to Melbourne, Australia, where his sister had settled with her Australian husband, but he returned to England two years later to begin his national service. During this time he learnt Russian, which would prove an asset during his literary career. In 1955 he went to New College, Oxford to read English, graduating with First Class honours in 1959. He married Maureen Skewes in 1958 and they had two children.

By this time he had begun writing verse. His first collection, *Personal and Possessive*, was published in 1964, and he was featured in *Penguin Modern Poets II* in 1968. Subsequent collections of his poetry included *Symphony in Moscow* (1974), and *Dreaming in Bronze* (1981). From 1959 to 1963 he taught English at Teignmouth Grammar School, and from 1963 to 1978 he was a lecturer in English at Hereford College of Education, where he was head of department for the last two years.

He left his teaching career to become a full-time writer, and after having 'roamed the border between prose and poetry' for some years, published his first novel, *The Flute Player*, in 1979. His third, *The White Hotel* (1981), the story of a woman undergoing psychoanalysis, became an international bestseller and was shortlisted for the Booker Prize. In his words, most of his novels 'deal with people caught up in the great, and mostly horrifying, historical events of our century.' *Flying in to Love* (1992) was a fictional treatment of the assassination of President Kennedy.

In 1987 he moved back to Cornwall. His first marriage had ended in divorce in 1976; his second, to Denise Aldred, ended with her death from cancer in 1998, and the following year he married Victoria Field. In addition to several collections of verse, novels, translations of Russian poetry by Yevtushenko, Pushkin and Akhmatova, he also published a biography, *Alexander Solzhenitsyn: a Century in his Life* (1998). His autobiography *Memories and Hallucinations* (1988) was an exercise in writing-as-therapy which followed his own experience of psychoanalysis after a nervous breakdown and 'writer's block'. In it he wrote of his early family environment being rather sheltered, as a result of which he spent much of the rest of his life catching up on what really goes on in the world. His first stage play, *Hell Fire Corner*, set in Cornwall at the beginning of the twentieth century, had its debut performance in the Hall for Cornwall, Truro in 2004.

In June 1993 he was invited to a party at William Golding's (q.v.) house nearby, and spent an enjoyable evening with his host. Next day he was shocked to learn that the elder man had died of a massive heart attack while getting ready for bed that night. Recalling the occasion some years later in *The Guardian*, Thomas remarked ruefully that he still treasured the author's last piece of writing – his phone number.

Thomas Tonkin

Antiquary and Scholar

Thomas Tonkin was born at Trevaunance, St Agnes, and baptised in the parish church there on 26 September 1678, the eldest son of Hugh Tonkin, landowner, and his first wife Frances. His father was vice-warden of the stannaries in 1701 and as sheriff of Cornwall in 1702. Thomas matriculated from Queen's College, Oxford in 1694, and became a student at Lincoln's Inn in February 1695. At Oxford he became a friend of Edmund Gibson, afterwards bishop of London, and Edward Lhuyd, whose work was regarded as the foundation of modern Celtic linguistic studies.

He is said to have become fluent in Welsh as well as Cornish. Tonkin and Lhuyd corresponded for several years after leaving Oxford; Lhuyd's pioneering studies were influential in the foundation of modern Celtic studies, and he undertook extensive research on aspects and origins of the Cornish language. Thanks to him, Tonkin became fluent not only in Cornish but also Welsh.

Tonkin returned to Cornwall in about 1700 to make an in-depth study of the county's history, topography and genealogy. He married Elizabeth Kempe of Penryn in about 1710 and they had several children, though the male line became extinct on the death of their third son, also named Thomas.

Shortly after the death of his father, it became evident that previous generations of his family had rather overreached themselves in spending much of the family fortune on improvements to the estate, notably the building of a quay at Trevaunance Porth, in Trevaunance Cove, to ship ore from the local mines. By 1710 he had spent a further £6,000 on the quay's upkeep and tried to raise money through launching a weekly market and fairs at St Agnes, but local opposition obstructed his schemes and he fell into debt. The quay at Trevaunance was destroyed in around 1730 after crumbling through years of poor maintenance. After falling into the hands of a creditor, Tonkin was the subject of legal action, lost the case, and had to sell the Trevaunance family estates. He spent the rest of his days at his wife's estate in Gorran parish.

Family influence, notably the patronage of his in-laws, helped him to win a by-election at Helston in April 1714. He only represented the borough at Westminster until January 1715. During his nine months in the House of Commons he took little part in parliamentary activity, preferring to devote his time to academic pursuits instead. In 1737 he intended to publish a three-volume history of Cornwall, priced at three guineas, and a collection of writings in Cornish, alongside his own translations into contemporary English. Due to his lack of finances, neither was ever published.

He died at Gorran and was buried in the local church on 4 January 1742. His extensive collection of material on the topography, natural history, parochial history, and language of Cornwall remained unpublished, but his work in recording the literary fragments of the dying Cornish language for posterity was appreciated by subsequent generations of scholars. His manuscripts were regularly used in research by others, some of whom obtained sections and donated them to the Museum of the Royal Institution of Cornwall.

Sheila Tracy

Musician, Broadcaster and Journalist

Sheila Tracy was born Sheila Lugg in Helston on 10 January 1934 and grew up in Mullion. Educated at Truro High School, she learnt the piano at six and violin at eight, spent four years at the Royal Academy of Music, and took up trombone as a third instrument in her second year, never having had a chance to learn a brass instrument at school. She joined the Ivy Benson All Girls Band in 1956, played in two summer seasons at the Villa Marina, Isle of Man, one-nighters at American bases in Britain, Germany, France, nightclubs in Dusseldorf, Amsterdam and Rotterdam, and the Chelsea Arts Ball, Royal Albert Hall on New Year's Eve, alongside Ted Heath and Humphrey Lyttelton. Next she formed a vocal/trombone duo with fellow trombonist Phyl Brown, the Tracy Sisters. They appeared in variety, cabaret, on radio and television, touring with Shirley Bassey and Max Bygraves, and broadcasting on *Workers Playtime*, *Midday Music Hall* and *Variety Parade*. After three months' cabaret in Calcutta at Christmas 1959, they were offered six months in Las Vegas but turned it down for family reasons, thus becoming probably the only act ever to turn down Vegas.

As a BBC TV announcer she appeared on several series including *Spoonful of Sugar, Music From Great Houses, Spotlight South West, Points West*, and *South Today*. In 1973 she joined Radio 4 as a staff announcer, and in 1974 became the first woman newsreader on the station. Transferring to Radio 2 in 1977, she presented *Big Band Special* from 1979 to 2001 and from 1987 introduced some fifty concerts a year with the BBC Big Band, including their tour of America in 1991 with guest George Shearing. Other shows for the network included the *National Big Band Competition* and *You and the Night and the Music*, but it was her *Truckers Hour* that gained her a certain notoriety as Citizen's Band radio was not yet legal.

I was using all the CB lingo and one night read out the CB for cheerio, goodbye, that was often on the end of the 200 or so letters a week that came rolling in. My engineer leapt two feet in the air saying, "I think you've just said something very rude". The Radio 2 Controller summoned me and said, "I'll have no hesitation in taking you off the air if you ever say anything like that again." "But I didn't know what it meant," I said. "You should have found out what it meant!" he replied. The CB sign off nearly everyone used was 'Keep the lipstick off the dipstick!' She also contributed regularly to Radio 4's *Breakaway*.

In the late 1970s she compered a series of brass band concerts at the Colston Hall, Bristol, and in 1994 was part of the first female adjudicating panel for the fourth division of the naional campionships. She has been at the Royal Albert Hall to announce the results of the National Finals since 1997, compering the gala concert that follows.

She presented *Swingtime with Sheila Tracy* on Primetime Radio from 2001 to 2006 and on Saga 106.6fm and Saga 105.7fm until Smooth Radio took over the company in April 2007. Her books include *Around Helston and the Lizard* (1980), *Who's who on Radio* (1983), *Who's Who in Popular Music* (1984), *Bands, Booze & Broads* (1995), on the American musicians in the swing era, and *Talking Swing* (1997), on their British counterparts. In 1997 she was made a Freeman of the City of London and an Associate of the Royal Academy of Music. In 2002 she was awarded the Alan Dell Trophy for services to music and in 2003 was honoured by the Big Band Academy of America, Los Angeles.

Miles Tredinnick

Author

Miles Tredinnick was born at RAF Padgate, Warrington, where his father Wing Cmmdr Reginald Tredinnick was stationed on 18 February 1955 but grew up in Falmouth. He was educated at Blundells School, trained as a photo-journalist in the Midlands and co-wrote a stage musical *Doomsday Genesis* with composer Keith Kerslake. After moving to London, he worked as a personal assistant to impresario Robert Stigwood.

In 1976 he formed the punk band London with drummer Jon Moss, bassist Steve Voice and guitarist Dave Wight. As vocalist and main songwriter, he took the name Riff Regan, Riff from a character in *West Side Story* and Regan from John Thaw's character in *The Sweeney*. Manager Simon Napier-Bell secured them a record deal with MCA Records and a nationwide tour supporting The Stranglers in the summer of 1977. Two singles *Everyone's A Winner* and *Animal Games*, an EP *Summer Of Love* and an album *Animal Games* were all produced by Napier-Bell at IBC Studios, London. They disbanded in December 1977 after a nationwide headlining tour and a farewell gig at the Marquee Club. Miles then recorded five solo singles as Riff Regan. In 1982 he co-wrote *The Hottest Woman In Town*, recorded by guitarist Bernie Torme.

He then left the music business and started writing comedy scripts. His first play *Because Of Mr Darrow*, produced at the Finborough Arms Theatre, London, was followed by *Laugh? I Nearly Went To Miami!* It had a successful London fringe run starring Russell Wootton and Jill Greenacre before being produced for the first Liverpool Festival of Comedy. Translated into several languages, it was performed all around the world, achieving particular success in Vienna where as ... *Und Morgen Fliegen Wir Nach*

Miami, it became one of the city's most popular stage plays. His other writing projects at this time included stage and television material for Frankie Howerd, including a special, *Superfrank*, for Channel 4, and an updated stage version of Howerd's popular television series *Up Pompeii!* and cartoon stories for the international *Walt Disney Magazine*.

In 1988 he created and wrote the BBC TV situation comedy *Wyatt's Watchdogs*, starring Brian Wilde and Trevor Bannister, leading to an invitation to write for the long-established BBC series *Birds of a Feather*. Another stage comedy, *It's Now or Never!*, starred Tony Roper, Peter Polycarpou, Heather Alexander, and Leyton Summers as Elvis Presley, and was followed by the thriller *Getting Away With Murder*, which had a successful run in Hampstead and was later published as *Twist*. A theatrical comedy, *Topless*, was a one-woman play set on an open-top London sightseeing bus. After director Martin Bailey's original production in 1999, it returned to the West End for a second season the following year. Produced by The Big Bus Co. and directed by the author, it was performed on top of a sightseeing bus driving through the streets of London, and its success led to the sequel, *Topless in Philadelphia*. In 2001 he published his first novel, *Fripp*, about a private investigator set largely in Cornwall.

As well as his writing commitments he worked for The Big Bus Co. for many years training tour guides in London, Dubai, Philadelphia and Baltimore. He sang in the rock band Magic Bus, and in 2008 reformed London with Steve Voice and two new musicians for further live work.

Joseph Treffry

Engineer, Mining Adventurer and Industrialist

Joseph Thomas Austen was baptised at St Andrew's Church, Plymouth, on 1 May 1782, son of Joseph Austen, brewer and former mayor of Plymouth, and his wife Susanna. He was educated at Exeter College, Oxford, but left without graduating. On his return he became involved in management of the Treffry family estate at Place, partly inherited by his mother, and tried to improve the estate farms' profitability by taking advantage of high wartime agricultural prices and adding further agricultural land. After 1815 he added to the estate's shareholdings in local copper and tin mines, and by 1820 he had acquired control of Wheal mines at Par, which he combined with neighbouring mines and renamed it Fowey Consols. It became one of the most productive mines in Cornwall, employing about 1,700 workers.

Such success owed much to his investment in good transport facilities, above all building and owning ships to handle the business and constructing a quay at Fowey. In 1828 he drew up plans for a new harbour at Par so larger vessels could dock there and service the mines without having to transport ore through Fowey. He built his own smelting works at Par, and the port was later linked by railway to the Luxulyan granite quarries, which he owned and developed. In 1833 the first shipments left Par harbour.

He opened another large copper mine, Par Consols, which came into production in 1840, and built a tramway to link it to the harbour. Up to fifty vessels of 200 tons could now be accommodated there, while larger vessels could anchor in the bay and have their cargoes transhipped by barge. He also constructed a canal from Ponts Mill and Fowey Consols mine to his new harbour which linked to a number of inclines leading to mines in the area. The minerals were brought down these cable inclines on wagons and loaded on to barges, with coal being brought up to fuel the pumping engines in the mines.

In 1836 he bought the pier and harbour of Newquay, ideally placed for shipping lead from the East Wheal Rose Mine, and china clay and stone from his quarries. He intended to build a horse-drawn tramway from Ponts Mill to Newquay, and work began in 1837 on the Ponts Mill to Bugle section, a viaduct near Luxulyan. It was built of stone from the Carbeans and Colcerrow quarries, between 1839 and 1842; they carried the tramway and also provided a high level leat across the Luxulyan Valley. The lines from the quarries to the viaduct were the first parts of the railway to be operational and completed in 1844. Later he tried to connect Cornwall with the growing national railway network; from 1844 to 1846 he was chairman of a provisional committee established to do so, and from 1846 to 1850 he presided over the Cornwall Railway Board.

After the death of his maternal uncle, William Treffry, he changed his name to Treffry by deed poll. In addition to restoring and developing the semi-derelict Place (pictured), he served as a magistrate and was high sheriff of Cornwall in 1838–9, a committee member of the East Cornwall Agricultural Society, a patron of the Tywardreath Gardening Society, and vice-president of the Royal Cornwall Polytechnic Society from 1849 until his death. He died at Place on 29 January 1850.

Sir Jonathan Trelawney

Bishop of Winchester

Jonathan Trelawney, third baronet, was born on 24 March 1650 at Trelawne, Pelynt, second of six surviving sons of Sir Jonathan Trelawney, 2nd Baronet and his wife, Mary, daughter of Sir Edward Seymour of Berry Pomeroy. He was educated at Westminster School and Christ Church, Oxford. In 1677 he was appointed a royal chaplain-extraordinary and granted the living of Calstock; after it was found to have been already granted to someone else, he was given the rectory of St Ives and his father presented him with the family living of South Hill. The parsonages of both needed rebuilding, so Trelawney lived at the family seat of Trelawne, over ten miles away from both.

His elder brother had died in October 1680, and he therefore inherited his father's debts as well as the title of third baronet in March 1681. At first much of his time was spent on local affairs, inspecting his father's old militia troop and succeeding him in his role of Vice-Admiral of south Cornwall in February 1682, and being named on the commission of the peace. In March 1684, he married Rebecca Hele.

When the Duke of York ascended the throne as James II in February 1685 and the Duke of Monmouth rebelled, he mobilised the Cornish militia. Expecting a suitable reward for his loyalty and services, he was disappointed to receive nothing more prestigious than the bishopric of Bristol. Despite his loyalty to the King, by 1687 he found himself increasingly opposed to his staunch Roman Catholicism. When called upon to sign an address of thanks for the declaration of indulgence granting toleration to dissenters and Roman Catholics in April 1687, and to promote it among his clergy, he did nothing about it for three weeks, then told his Bristol clergy that he would not sign the address personally, though when he met them later they followed his lead and also demurred, he claimed that only their reluctance had prompted him to refrain from signing.

In May 1688 he supported the petition of Sancroft and five other bishops against the order to read the declaration of indulgence in churches, and was one of the seven bishops prosecuted by the King, who charged them with inciting rebellion, but they were acquitted. Believing Trelawney still loyal to him, the King appointed him Bishop of Exeter. In November when Trelawney's brother Charles, a senior army officer, defected to the Prince of Orange (shortly to become King William III), Trelawney sent his own assurance of loyalty to the King.

On 5 December, while Trelawney was at Bristol, the Earl of Shrewsbury arrived with a regiment of foot and a letter from the Prince of Orange. Trelawney replied cautiously, expressing approval for steps taken to secure the Protestant religion, plus England's laws and liberties. James's flight abroad temporarily delayed Trelawney's translation to Exeter. A few weeks later he voted against the notion that James II had abdicated, and against the offer of the crown to William and Mary. Nevertheless he did not reject the subsequent settlement, and took the oaths, and as a result the new sovereigns endorsed and expedited his translation to Exeter.

He died at his home in Chelsea on 19 July 1721, and his body was returned to Cornwall for burial in the family vault at Pelynt Church.

Henry Trengrouse

Inventor

Henry Trengrouse was born at Helston on 18 March 1772, the son of Nicholas and Mary Trengrouse. Educated at Helston Grammar School, he then became a cabinet maker.

His practical skills were soon to be put to far more valuable use. While out walking near Mount's Bay on 24 December 1807 he saw the 44-gun warship *Anson* being driven onto the coast during a storm. It had left Falmouth and reached Ushant, off the Breton coast, when bad weather forced it to turn back. The captain mistook the Lizard for Falmouth, and in making for land 60yds from shore the vessel overturned. Its broken masts formed a bridge to the shore, and some sailors managed to use them to reach the shore, but over 120 men were drowned as they could not make the short distance from the wreck to the shore because of the boiling surf. This spurred him to find a way to save the lives of shipwrecked seafarers. Initially he intended to build a lifeboat, but then decided to concentrate on life-saving apparatus instead.

Later while he was watching a firework display on Helston Green to celebrate King George III's birthday, he decided a rocket-powered line might provide the solution. His thought was that if lightweight rockets were put on the ships, grounded ships could help themselves; the rockets accelerated gradually, so the line would not snap. In an onshore gale, the most likely scenario with a grounded ship, the rocket would be carried by the wind to the shore which was an easy target to hit.

Another inventor, George Manby, was simultaneously working on a similar system, but Trengrouse's method, which he completed in 1808, was considered superior. In February 1818 he demonstrated his apparatus to Admiral Sir Charles Rowley, a senior naval officer of the day. One month later a committee reported that his method appeared the best that had been suggested for the purpose of saving lives from shipwreck by gaining a communication with the shore. It was also suggested that a specimen apparatus should be placed in every dockyard so that naval officers would become familiar with its methods. A committee of the elder brethren of Trinity House seconded this proposal and recommended that it should be carried on all vessels.

His invention was ignored by the government, but the Russian ambassador invited him to St Petersburg to develop the invention, though he was too patriotic to consider putting his services at the disposal of a foreign power. The British government then ordered twenty sets, but decided to have them constructed by the Ordnance department, and paid Trengrouse £50 compensation. In 1821 the Society of Arts awarded him their silver medal and thirty guineas, but these were the only rewards he ever received for his work. He spent the rest of his life in virtual poverty, died at Helston on 14 February 1854 and was buried at St Michael's Church, Helston.

Silvanus Trevail

Architect

Silvanus Trevail was born in Luxulyan in October 1851. A brief period of activity in local government affairs led to his serving for a while on Cornwall County Council in the Liberal interest. He also became Mayor of Truro, and President of the Society of Architects.

With railway expansion in the 1870s connecting the coastal towns of the South West to the holidaying middle classes, who all had time and money to take in the sea air, he planned to make Cornwall the rival of the resorts on the south coast. In 1890 he formed the Cornish Hotels Co. in order to create a chain of first class hotels, whose guests could move between them at a whim. Lack of funds hampered his plans and he was forced to settle with just one hotel, the Atlantic. Nevertheless he decided he would try and develop the headlands of Newquay with the aim of turning them into an upmarket estate, the whole scheme incorporating a luxury hotel called the Headland. The scheme aroused fierce opposition in the town, culminating in civil disturbances which came to be known as the 'Newquay riots'. The proposed site of the hotel had previously been used as land on which the local farmers grazed their livestock and local fishermen dried their nets. They were angry with Trevail's proposals, which they felt threatened to ruin their livelihoods.

Despite local opposition, work on the Headland Hotel began in August 1897. Outraged farmers and fishermen rushed to the site, where they tore down the wooden works office. Valuable tools and planks of wood were hurled off the cliff. When Trevail returned to the site the following day, the mob were waiting. Missiles, including eggs and apples were hurled at him, before he was pinned to the railing and subjected as the press reported, to a 'very fierce outpouring of contempt and insolent abuse.' Although hundreds took part in the demonstration, only twenty-two men were charged, and fined £2 each for committing malicious damage to goods. Construction continued, although local workers were reluctant to return to the site and unemployed miners from Redruth had to be employed instead.

He had never been strong, and his health was further undermined by depression. On 7 November 1903 he travelled on the Cornishman Express on the Great Western Railway from Truro, having booked to St Austell to attend the funeral of a relative. Between Lostwithiel and Bodmin Road, the report of a gun was heard. When a guard went to inspect, he found Trevail's body in the lavatory with a shot through the head and a revolver lying by his side.

Richard Trevithick

Inventor

Richard Trevithick was born in Tregajorran, near Illogan, on 13 April 1771, and educated at Camborne School. As a young man he was known as the Cornish giant as he was 6ft 2in tall, and renowned as one of the best wrestlers in Cornwall.

While working with his father at Wheal Treasury Mine, he revealed some skills as an engineer, and was promoted to engineer of the Ding Dong Mine at Penzance. While there he developed a successful high-pressure engine much in demand locally for raising the ore and refuse from mines. He also began experimenting with producing a steam locomotive, and by 1796 had produced a miniature vehicle. Next he built a larger steam road locomotive, known as the *Puffing Billy*, which he used on Christmas Eve 1801 to take friends on a short journey. It could not travel long distances as he never found a way to keep up the steam for any length of time. Despite these setbacks he travelled to London and showed it to several leading scientists.

In 1803 the company Vivian & West agreed to finance his experiments, and he exhibited his new locomotive in London, but after some technical problems the company withdrew their backing. He then found another sponsor in Samuel Homfray, owner of ironworks at Merthyr Tydfil. In February 1804 he produced the world's first steam engine to run successfully on rails, the *Penydarren*, which managed to haul 10 tons of iron, seventy passengers and five wagons from Penydarren ironworks at to the Merthyr-Cardiff Canal. On a nine-mile journey it reached speeds of nearly 5mph, but it was so heavy it broke the cast iron rails and only made three journeys. Deciding it was not viable, Homfray decided to abandon the project. Next Trevithick was employed by Christopher Blackett, owner of a colliery in Northumberland, needing a locomotive to replace the horse-drawn coal wagons on his five-mile wooden wagonway which took the coal from Wylam to the River Tyne. Again, the experiment failed as the Wylam locomotive proved too heavy for Blackett's wooden wagonway.

He then returned to Cornwall and developed a new locomotive; in the summer of 1808 he erected a circular railway in Euston Square and during the months of July and August people could ride his locomotive on the payment of 1s. It reached speeds of 12 mph but again the rails broke and he had to end the experiment. Without financial backing, he had to abandon his plans to develop a steam locomotive. Next he found work with a company who paid him to develop a steam dredger to lift waste from the bottom of the Thames, and was paid 6d for every ton lifted from the river.

In 1816 he went to work as an engineer in a silver mine in Peru, where his steam-engines were successful and he used his profits to acquire his own silver mines. When war broke out in 1826 he was forced to flee, leaving behind his steam engines and silver mines. After working in Costa Rica he moved to Columbia, where he met Robert Stephenson, who was building a railway in that country and who financed Trevithick's return to England. He continued to work on new ideas, including the propulsion of steamboats by means of a spiral wheel at the stern, an improved marine boiler, a new recoil gun carriage, apparatus for heating apartments, and the building of a 1,000ft cast-iron column to commemorate the 1832 Reform Act but they received no financial support. He died in poverty at Dartford on 22 April 1833.

Paul Tyler

Politician

Paul Archer Tyler was born on 29 October 1941 in south Devon. Through his mother he was a direct descendant of Bishop Jonathan Trelawney (q.v.), while his father's family were descended from Oliver Cromwell. In 1964 he was elected Britain's youngest county councillor. He was vice-chairman of the Dartmoor National Park Committee and a member of the Devon & Cornwall Police Authority.

In 1968 he was selected to contest the Bodmin constituency and stood there at the 1970 general election, but lost to the Conservatives. At the February 1974 election he won by a majority of only nine, and was appointed House of Commons spokesman on housing, transport and rate reform. At the October election that year he increased the Liberal vote, though the Conservatives narrowly regained the seat, holding it with an increased majority when he stood again at the 1979 general election.

He was Managing Director of the *Cornwall Courier* local newspaper group from 1976 to 1981, and presenter of BBC South West TV *Discovery* series in 1978. In 1982 he contested the Beaconsfield by-election, where he pushed the Labour candidate, Tony Blair, into third place, with a lost deposit. In the 1983 election he was David Steel's campaign organiser, and elected Chairman of the Liberal Party 1983-6. He was Campaign Adviser to David Steel and member of the Alliance Planning Group 1986-7, and member of the campaign team in the 1987 general election. In 1985 he was awarded the CBE for political services. As Liberal Democrat candidate for the Cornwall and Plymouth constituency in the European Parliament election in 1989, he reduced the

Conservative majority and gained the highest ever Liberal or Liberal Democrat vote at the time and the best result in the country. In 1992 he was elected Liberal Democrat Member for North Cornwall. Back in Parliament he served the Liberal Democrat Front Bench as Chief Whip, Shadow Leader of the House and Liberal Democrat spokesman on rural affairs, agriculture and transport.

After the 1997 election he was elected Liberal Democrat Chief Whip, and had a prominent role in rural and food industry issues, promoting the Organic Food and Family Targets Bill in 2000 and covering all aspects of the foot-and-mouth epidemic in the early months of 2001, working with farming and other organisations to seek more effective government action. He also worked closely with the Youth Hostels Association and the British Resorts Association, and was an active member of the Royal British Legion Gulf War Group.

He retired from the House of Commons at the 2005 general election, was created Baron Tyler of Linkinhorne, and was appointed a Deputy Lieutenant of Cornwall in February 2006. As Liberal Democrat spokesman in the Lords on constitutional reform issues, he served on the 2006 Joint Committee on Conventions, which examined and set out the relationship between the House of Lords and the House of Commons.

In 2007 he confirmed his support for a Cornish Assembly when interviewed regarding proposals for a Constitutional Convention. As befitted a man who wore yellow-and-black striped socks, the Cornish colours, he was a forceful opponent of rules which prevented the St Piran's flag from flying across Cornwall without specific permission. He branded the regulations a 'mind-boggling absurdity', saying it was 'a reprehensible betrayal of the former Minister's commitment to fairness' that exemptions were still made for St David of Wales, St Andrew of Scotland and St George of England, and for every other national flag', but not that of Cornwall.

Alfred Wallis

Painter

Alfred Wallis was born on 18 August 1855 in Devonport. His parents, Charles and Jane Wallis, were from Penzance in Cornwall and had moved to Devonport to find work in 1850 where Alfred and his brother Charles were born. Soon afterwards their mother died and the family moved back to Penzance. After leaving school Alfred became an apprentice basket maker and then a mariner in the merchant service, a job which involved sailing schooners across the North Atlantic between Penzance and Newfoundland.

He married Susan Ward at Penzance in 1876, when he was twenty, his wife was forty-one, and became stepfather to her five children. He continued his life as a deep-sea fisherman on the Newfoundland run in the early days of his marriage, which brought him a good wage until the death of his two infant children, after which he took up fishing and general labouring jobs in Penzance. In 1890 they moved to St Ives, where he established himself as a marine stores dealer, buying scrap iron, sails, rope and other items. In 1912 his business closed, but he continued to earn a living doing odd jobs and working for a local antiques dealer, Mr Armour, which gave him some knowledge of and insight into the world of *objets d'art*.

When his wife died in 1922 he took up painting as a hobby or, as he later said, to keep himself company. He had never had any formal training, and his paintings are an excellent example of naïve art, with perspective being ignored and an object's scale often based on its relative importance in the scene. His seascapes were painted largely from memory, mainly because the world of sail he had known as a younger man was being replaced by steamships. In retrospect he is thought of as Britain's foremost twentieth-century 'primitive' painter, and was regarded by some as a Cornish equivalent of the naïve French artist Henri 'Douanier' Rousseau. As he had little money to spend on materials, he painted on whatever flat surfaces were to hand, generally using cardboard torn from packing boxes or pieces of driftwood, using a limited palette of paint bought from ships' chandlers.

In 1928, a few years after he had begun to paint, fellow artists Ben Nicholson and Christopher Wood came to visit the other like-minded souls at St Ives. They were fascinated by Wallis and his unsophisticated approach. He soon found himself involved, perhaps none too willingly, with a circle of the some of most progressive artists working in Britain in the 1930s. Nevertheless it had no effect on his style or methods, as he never altered his approach to painting. He was always regarded as a somewhat lonely but fiercely independent man.

Through Nicholson and Wood he was introduced to dealer Jim Ede, who undertook to promote his work in London. Nevertheless he sold very few paintings during his lifetime, and continued to live in poverty until his death in the Madron Workhouse, Penzance, on 29 August 1942. He was buried in Barnoon Cemetery, overlooking the Tate St Ives Gallery. An elaborate gravestone, depicting a small mariner at the foot of a large lighthouse, a popular feature in many of Wallis's paintings, was made from tiles by the potter Bernard Leach (q.v.).

Samuel Wallis

Naval Officer and Pacific Explorer

Samuel Wallis was born near Camelford, son of John Wallis and Sarah Barrett, and baptised on 23 April 1728 at Lanteglos. He joined the navy, becoming a midshipman and master's mate before receiving his commission as lieutenant in 1748. After serving on several ships from 1753 onwards, he was appointed commander of the sloop *Swan* in 1756. In April 1757 he was given command of the frigate *Port Mahon*, and in September 1758 the *Prince of Orange*. The following year he took part in the Quebec campaign under Vice-Admiral Charles Saunders, then returned with his ship to Europe for service in the Seven Years' War, in which hostilities were not concluded until 1763.

In June 1766 he was instructed by the Earl of Egmont, First Lord of the Admiralty, to take command of an expedition in search of the continent Terra Australis Incognita in the south Pacific. The frigate *Dolphin* had just returned from a world voyage under Commodore John Byron, who had sailed through the Tuamotu Archipelago in French Polynesia in June 1765 and was certain that an as yet uncharted land mass to the south existed. Wallis sailed on 21 August 1766, accompanied by Philip Carteret, in the decrepit, slower sloop *Swallow*.

Once he was clear of the Strait of Magellan in April 1767, Wallis followed his instructions to sail westwards from Cape Horn. On 6 June he reached the Tuamotu, where he saw five islands previously unrecognized by European explorers. Eleven days later he saw the first of the Society Islands at Mehetia, and the next day Tahiti, where the *Dolphin* stayed for five weeks. On the journey many of the crew had been stricken with fever and most of them soon recovered, though Wallis and his first lieutenant were taken ill with an unidentified illness described as 'a bilious disorder'. An ailing Wallis, in no state to exercise his authority as commander, had to rely mainly on George Robertson, the experienced shipmaster, and Tobias Furneaux, second lieutenant. The situation called for firm leadership as there had been violence shortly after the *Dolphin*'s arrival, and cannon fire to restore law and order left several casualties, dead and wounded, among the Tahitians.

Wallis and Robertson also considered that the island must be an outlying territory of the as yet more or less unknown southern continent, and in July 1767 the *Dolphin* sailed from Tahiti on a westerly course. They sighted more uncharted islands on their journey northwest towards the north Pacific, and home by way of Tinian, Batavia, and the Cape, reaching England in the last week of May 1768.

Altogether Wallis had discovered and charted fifteen islands, although this included several very small atolls. Poor health had done little to prevent him from laying the groundwork which would be of value to Captain Cook in preparing his famous voyage of exploration on board *Endeavour*. A number of the measures Cook adopted for the well-being of his crews had been put into practice by Wallis, who had attempted to improve their diet by obtaining fresh vegetables and fruit, ensuring their clothes and bedding were kept dry and clean, introducing a three-watch system so they would all have reasonable periods of rest. He was regarded as a humane and conscientious leader, always doing his best for the welfare of those below him.

Soon after his return he was awarded a grant of £525 in recognition of his work. In November 1770 he was given command of the *Torbay*, and later of the *Queen*. He died on 21 January 1795 at his home in Devonshire Street, Portland Place, London.

Virginia Woolf

Author

Adeline Virginia Stephen was born in London on 25 January 1882 to Sir Leslie Stephen and Julia Princep Duckworth and educated by her parents at their home, Hyde Park Gate, Kensington. Nevertheless she had a lifelong Cornish connection, as during the first twelve years of her life the family took their holidays at Talland House.

This late Victorian villa was situated on the edge of St Ives, above Porthminster Beach, with spectacular views across St Ives Bay towards Godrevy Lighthouse. Guests who stayed with the Woolfs on their holidays included her father's friends George Meredith, Ralph Waldo Emerson, James Russell Lowell, Henry James, and the young Rupert Brooke. In his biography of his aunt, Quentin Bell stated that St Ives 'provided [for her] a treasury of reminiscent gold from which she drew again and again' and called Cornwall 'the Eden of her youth, an unforgettable paradise.'

They leased the property annually for the purpose from the Great Western Railway Co., until Mrs Stephen's death in 1895. Nevertheless the memory of St Ives had a lifelong impact on her imagination and her writing, and it provided settings for two of her novels, *Jacob's Room* (1922), and *The Waves* (1931). Godrevy Lighthouse inspired *To The Lighthouse* (1927), which was largely autobiographical, and which she called 'easily the best of my books'. Although the story is set in the Isle of Skye, the house mentioned was in fact based on Talland House, and her descriptions of the lighthouse, the sea and the gardens leading down to it are based on the same features around St Ives Bay.

In *A Sketch of the Past*, an autobiographical essay which she wrote in 1939 and which was published posthumously, she portrayed the warm smells of a Cornish seaside garden, the long-gone Victorian tennis court, the clunk of cricket balls on the lawn and the trickle of the fountain hedged in by 'damp evergreens', smell the wild roses and the grapes and peaches which hung in the ornate greenhouses.

She also described her father's discovery of Talland House, when he found St Ives on one of his walking tours, around 1881, stayed there, and saw the property to let. In retrospect, she considered, nothing was quite so important to them as children as the annual summer in Cornwall, when they could listen to the waves breaking on the shore, go digging in the sand, sailing in a fishing boat:

> ... to scrabble over the rocks and see the red and yellow anemones flourishing their antennae; or stuck like blobs of jelly to the rock; to find a small fish flapping in a pool; to pick up cowries; to look over the grammar in the dining room and see the lights changing on the bay; the leaves of the escallonia grey or bright green.' As for St Ives, it 'gave me all the pure delight which is before my eyes, even at this moment.

After years of suffering from depression, she committed suicide on 28 March 1941 by drowning herself in the River Ouse near her Sussex home, Monk's House, Rodmell.

Brenda Wootton

Folk Singer

Brenda Ellery was born in London, in her own words an accident of birth she regretted, on 10 February 1928. Raised as she said, 'on a basinful of chapel and a bucketful of superstition', she grew up in Newlyn, where her vocal ability was soon recognised. She began her musical career while still at school, singing in village halls throughout west Cornwall. This led to her becoming active on the folk scene and almost single-handedly kept the Cornish folk-song tradition alive for many years, and she became the first singer to give public performances of songs in the Cornish language outside Cornwall.

In 1948 she married John Wootton. She made her debut as a soloist at Cornwall's first folk music club, the Count House at Botallack, where she worked with John the Fish and the then little-known Ralph McTell. Her first recordings, two songs with John, appeared on the album *More Singing at the Count House*, recorded there in November 1965. Later she opened her own club, the Pipers Folk Club, at St Buryan.

Her career as a professional singer took off later in the decade when she recorded several albums on Cornwall's Sentinel label, including *Pasties and Cream*, with John the Fish, *Starry Gazey Pie*, and *No Song to Sing*, both with Robert Bartlett, *Crowdy Crawn* and *Way Down to Lamorna*. Her repertoire over the years covered folk, rock, blues, jazz and even hymns, though she was best remembered for her Cornish 'standards' such as *Lamorna*, *The White Rose*, *Camborne Hill*, *The Stratton Carol* and the ballads *Mordonnow* and *Tamar*. She considered herself equally at home when singing in Cornish, Breton or English.

She made several appearances on BBC TV and radio, and for a while was a presenter on BBC Radio Cornwall's *Sunday Choice*. Although she never became well known on the national folk scene in Britain, she was very popular in France, where she toured regularly and where her album *Lyonnesse* topped the album charts. In Brittany she was always in demand, and appeared in the first ever Lorient Interceltic Festival. The possessor of a sense of the ridiculous, she became friends with President Mitterrand and his family, and would often say, 'When I'm with them, I think to myself, if only my mother could see me now.' She was a Bard of the Cornish Gorsedd, where she was known by her Bardic name of Gwylan Gwavas (Seagull of Newlyn). She also performed throughout Europe and as far afield as Australia. Fiercely proud of her county, she always started her performances with the words, 'I'm from Cornwall.'

Her greatest disappointment came when ill-health prevented her from sharing the stage at the bicentennial celebrations of the French Revolution in 1989 with the American soprano, Jessye Norman. After a long illness she died at her Penzance home on 11 March 1994. A tribute concert featured performances from John the Fish, Ralph McTell, Decameron and Michael Chapman, and was later released on video as *Brenda's Friends.*